A Brief Historical Survey of Marian Devotion and Theology

Fr. Peter Samuel Kucer, MSA

En Route Books and Media, LLC
5705 Rhodes Avenue
St. Louis, MO 63109

Cover credit: TJ Burdick

Library of Congress Control Number: 2017956385

ISBN-10:0-9994704-0-X
ISBN-13: 978-0-9994704-0-4

DEDICATION

In memory of my mother, Roberta Kucer, who instilled in me a love of study and a love of her people, the chosen people.

In addition, I dedicate this book to the members of my community, the Missionaries of the Holy Apostles.

ACKNOWLEDGMENTS

I would particularly like to acknowledge Fr. Isaac Martinez, MSA, former General of the Missionaries of the Holy Apostles, who gave me permission to publish, and Bishop Christian Rodembourg, MSA, who as the first MSA to be ordained a bishop brought our MSA charism into a deeper ecclesial dimension by assuming the office of bishop the year this book was published.

Special thanks to Dr. Sebastian Mahfood, OP, president of En Route Books and Media, for publishing this work.

Fr. Peter Samuel Kucer, MSA

CONTENTS

1

[1] Web Gallery of Art, "The Virgin in Prayer, Giovanni Battista Salvi da Sassoferrato (1609-1685), *Jungfrun i bön* (1640-1650). National Gallery, London," photograph,

Mary, Mother of God & Mother of the Church

Chapter 1

Foreshadowing of the Old Testament

Part I: Theology of Women

Introduction

Vatican II's Dogmatic Constitution on Divine Revelation, *Dei Verbum*, teaches that "God, the inspirer and author of both Testaments, wisely arranged the New Testament to be hidden in the Old and the Old be manifest in the New."[2] Marian doctrines, therefore, are hidden in the Old Testament. Before seeing how Old Testament aspects that foreshadow and prepare for Mary are fulfilled in the New Testament, we will look at the Old Testament's theology of women in which Mary lays

---

https://commons.wikimedia.org/wiki/File%3ASassoferrato_-_Jungfrun_i_b%C3%B6n.jpg, (accessed July 29, 2016).

[2] Vatican II, "Dei Verbum, November 18, 1965," no. 16, Vatican.va, http://www.vatican.va/archive/hist_councils/ii_vatican_council/documents/vat-ii_const_19651118_dei-verbum_en.html, (accessed May 23, 2016).

hidden. First, we will examine how men and women both reflect God's infinite perfections. Then, shifting our attention to women only, we will look at key women and feminine images from the Old Testament which anticipate Mary's role in salvation history. This will include fertile and infertile women, powerless women, powerful women, the woman of Genesis chapter three, Miriam and Daughter Zion.

3

Men and Women Reflecting the Infinite Perfections of God

Along with being rooted in the Old Testament

---

3 Web Gallery of Art, "The *Creation of Eve*, from the Sistine Chapel ceiling by Michelangelo," photograph, https://commons.wikimedia.org/wiki/File%3AMichelangelo%2C_Creation_of_Eve_01.jpg, (accessed June 26, 2016).

theology of creation, Marian theology is also grounded in a theology of women. Old Testament theology of women rejects the polytheistic understanding of male and female partner Gods. This polytheism was expressed liturgically in pagan religions by men frequenting temples to engage in "sacred" sex with women to whom they were not married. In contrast, explains Joseph Ratzinger, the Old Testament vigorously rejects such ritual intercourse.[4] Deuteronomy 23:17 asserts that, "None of the daughters of Israel shall be a temple prostitute." (NRSV)

In describing the Babylonian custom of temple prostitution, the Greek historian Herodotus (c. 484–425 BC) writes:

> The foulest Babylonian custom is that which compels every woman of the land to sit in the temple of Aphrodite and have intercourse with some stranger once in her life. Many women who are rich and proud and disdain to mingle with the rest, drive to the temple in covered carriages drawn by teams, and stand there with a great retinue of attendants. But most sit down in the sacred plot of Aphrodite, with crowns of cord on

---

[4] Joseph Ratzinger, *Daughter Zion: Meditations on the Church's Marian Belief*, trans. McDermott (San Francisco: Ignatius Press, 1983), 14-15.

their heads; there is a great multitude of women coming and going;
passages marked by line run every
way through the crowd, by which the
men pass and make their choice.
Once a woman has taken her place
there, she does not go away to her
home before some stranger has cast
money into her lap, and had
intercourse with her outside the
temple; but while he casts the
money, he must say, "I invite you in
the name of Mylitta" (that is the
Assyrian name for Aphrodite). It
does not matter what sum the
money is; the woman will never
refuse, for that would be a sin, the
money being by this act made
sacred. So she follows the first man
who casts it and rejects no one. After
their intercourse, having discharged
her sacred duty to the goddess, she
goes away to her home; and there-
after there is no bribe however great
that will get her. So then the women
that are fair and tall are soon free to
depart, but the uncomely have long
to wait because they cannot fulfill
the law; for some of them remain for
three years, or four. There is a

custom like this in some parts of Cyprus.[5]

While the Israelites reject the notion of a woman goddess who serves as a companion of Yahweh, women were included in their under-standing of God in other ways. This is evident in Eve who, Genesis describes, along with Adam, was made in the image and likeness of God. "So God created humankind in his image, in the image of God he created them; male and female he created them." (Genesis 1: 27 NRSV) In affirming that certain of God's perfections can be described with feminine images, the *Catechism of the Catholic Church* states:

> By calling God "Father", the language of faith indicates two main things: that God is the first origin of everything and transcendent authority; and that he is at the same time goodness and loving care for all his children. God's parental tenderness can also be expressed by the image of motherhood, which emphasizes God's im-manence, the intimacy between Creator and creature. The language of faith thus draws on the human experience of parents, who are in a

---

[5] Herodotus, "The Histories," A.D. Godley, Ed. book 1, chapter 199, perseus.tufts.edu, http://www.perseus.tufts.edu/hopper/text?doc=Hdt.+1.199, (accessed May 23, 2016). The following citation is at the end of the quoted text. Herodotus, with an English translation by A. D. Godley. Cambridge. Harvard University Press. 1920.

way the first representatives of God for man. But this experience also tells us that human parents are fallible and can disfigure the face of fatherhood and motherhood. We ought therefore to recall that God transcends the human distinction between the sexes. He is neither man nor woman: he is God. He also transcends human fatherhood and motherhood, although he is their origin and standard: no one is father as God is Father.[6]

Notice that the Catechism calls God Father and does not simply attribute fatherly qualities to God. The Catechism is not saying that God is like a human father but rather that God is Father. In other words, the term Father is not being applied metaphorically to God but actually to God by way of analogy. Aquinas explains this as follows:

> A name is applied to that wherein is perfectly contained its whole signification, before it is applied to that which only partially contains it; for the latter bears the name by reason of a kind of similitude to that which answers perfectly to the signification of the name; since all imperfect things are taken from perfect things. Hence this name

---

[6] "The Catechism of the Catholic Church," no. 239, Vatican.va, http://www.vatican.va/archive/ccc_css/archive/catechism/p1s2c1p2.htm, (accessed May 23, 2016).

"lion" is applied first to the animal containing the whole nature of a lion, and which is properly so called, before it is applied to a man who shows something of a lion's nature, as courage, or strength, or the like; and of whom it is said by way of similitude.

Now it is manifest from the fore-going (27, 2; 28, 4), that the perfect idea of paternity and filiation is to be found in God the Father, and in God the Son, because one is the nature and glory of the Father and the Son. But in the creature, filiation is found in relation to God, not in a perfect manner, since the Creator and the creature have not the same nature; but by way of a certain likeness, which is the more perfect the nearer we approach to the true idea of filiation. For God is called the Father of some creatures, by reason only of a trace, for instance of irrational creatures, ... Therefore it is plain that "paternity" is applied to God first, as importing regard of one Person to another Person, before it imports the regard of God to creatures.[7]

In simpler language, 'God is father' is an analogy, similar to 'God is good' is an analogy. In the case of goodness and Fatherhood, they apply literally, or in the first, fullest sense to God, and only analogously, similarity with a greater difference, to us.[8] Although in reality fatherhood is first

---

[7] Thomas Aquinas, "Summa Theologica," I, Q. 33. Art. 3, newadvent.org, http://www.newadvent.org/summa/ 1033.htm#article3, (accessed May 24, 2016).

[8] Phillip Cary, *The History of Christian Theology* Lectures 1-18 (Chantilly: The Great Courses, 2008), 233, 240. As I explain in another lecture on Eastern Civilization by first quoting from the Fourth Lateran Council:

When, therefore, the Truth prays to the Father for those faithful to him saying I wish that *they may be one in us just as we are one*, this word one mean for the faithful a union of love in grace, and for the divine persons a unity of identify in nature, as the Truth say elsewhere, *You must be perfect as your heavenly Father is perfect*, as if he were to say more plainly, *You must be perfect* in the perfection of grace, *just as your Father is perfect* in the perfection that is his by nature, each in his own way. For between creator and creature there can be noted no similarity so great that a greater dissimilarity cannot be seen between them. (Norman P. Tanner, *Decrees of the Ecumenical Councils*, Volume I (Washington, DC: Georgetown University Press, 1990), 232.)

This passage from the Fourth Lateran Council has frequently been cited in reference to the Catholic concept of the Analogy of Being. As explained by St. Thomas Aquinas, the created world is related to the world by an analogy of being called an analogy of attribution. According to this analogy of attribution, God is the primary instance of being while all else is a

in God, we gain experiential knowledge of 'father' first from our human fathers before understanding God as father. For this reason, it is important to grasp why God is father. God's fatherhood is perfect because the Son He eternally generates is of the same nature as He is. In contrast, human sons only resemble the nature of their father. Human fatherhood is, consequently, an imperfect image of the purely spiritual Fatherhood of God. As the Catechism explains:

> In no way is God in man's image. He is neither man nor woman. God is pure spirit in which there is no place

---

secondary analogate of being. In other words, the relationship of God and his creation is not B is to G-C where being is B and G an C represent God and his creation. This would make being more fundamental than God himself. Neither is the relationship of God and creation G=C. This is monism. Nor is the relationship of God and creation G ≠ D in such a manner that creation has no relationship to God since he is totally transcendent. Instead, since God's essence (His whatness from the Latin verb *esse* meaning to be) is his existence (*esse ipse subsistens*) while the essence of anything else (*esse commune*) does not necessarily indicate it exists, this means that God is being (*esse*) while we, along with all of creation, only have being (*esse commune*)."

Esse ipse subsistence means that God's being (essence/whatness) is by itself existing and is the cause of all else that exists (*esse commune*). Esse commune but depends on God for existence. It does so by participating in perfections of God but not in God's essence. Thomas Joseph White, *The Analogy of Being: Invention of the Antichrist or the Wisdom of God?* (Grand Rapids: Wm. B. Eerdmans, 2011), 231.

for the difference between the sexes. But the respective "perfections" of man and woman reflect something of the infinite perfection of God: those of a mother and those of a father and husband.[9]

Ratzinger identifies feminine, motherly perfections that are reflected in the infinite perfection of God as wisdom. He writes:

In both Hebrew and Greek, "wisdom" is a feminine noun, and this is no empty grammatical phenomenon in antiquity's vivid awareness of language. "Sophia", a feminine noun, stands on that side of reality which is represented by the woman, by what is purely and simply feminine. It signifies the answer which emerges from the divine call of creation and election. It expresses precisely this: that there is a pure answer and that God's love finds its irrevocable dwelling place within it. In order to deal with the full complexity of the facts of the case, one must certainly consider that the word for "Spirit" in Hebrew (not, however, in Greek) is

---

[9] "Catechism of the Catholic Church," no. 370, Vatican.va, http://www.vatican.va/archive/ENG0015/__P1B.HTM, (accessed May 24, 2016).

feminine. In that respect, because of the teaching about the Spirit, one can as it were practically have a presentiment of the primordial type of the feminine, in a mysterious, veiled manner, within God himself.[10]

The Old Testament wisdom literature, therefore, according to Ratzinger, describes feminine perfections that are mysteriously, simply and primordially in God. Since in Greek 'theology' literally means words or language about God, Old Testament theology, specifically in its Wisdom Literature, includes and does not exclude women.[11]

Infertile-Fertile Pairs of Women

So far, we have glanced at the Old Testament theology of women with respect to Eve, made in the image and likeness of God, and the role of Wisdom (Sophia, in Greek, and Hokmot, in Hebrew). We will now see how the Old Testament theology of women is evident in women besides Eve.

Ratzinger points out that that alongside the patriarchs, women played a critical role in salvation history. He identifies three pairs of women who

---

[10] Joseph Ratzinger, *Daughter Zion: Meditations on the Church's Marian Belief*, trans. McDermott (San Francisco: Ignatius Press, 1983), 26-27.

[11] Ratzinger, J. (1983). *Daughter Zion: Meditations on the Church's Marian Belief*. (J. M. McDermott, Trans.) (p. 14). San Francisco: Ignatius Press.

prepared the way for Mary's role. These pairs are Sarah and Hagar, Rachel and Leah, and Hannah and Peninnah.[12] In all of these pairs, the first woman struggles with infertility while the second woman is fertile. Despite the Old Testament repeated affirmation of fertility as a blessing of God, the infertile woman is the one who receives a greater blessing by God. Sarah gives birth to Isaac, the father of Jacob, who became the father of the twelve sons/tribes of Israel. Rachel gives birth to Joseph, who saves his people from starvation. Hannah gives birth to the last of the Judges and great prophet Samuel.[13]

Powerless and Powerful Women

Similar to the infertile-fertile theme, another theme involving women also plays out in the Old Testament. This theme contrasts the powerless with the powerful. As God blessed the previously mentioned infertile women, so too does God bless a number of powerless women who faced powerful men. These powerless women include Deborah,

---

[12] Ratzinger does not include Rebekah since, unlike the other patriarchs, her husband Isaac did not have concubines. Consequently, there is a fertile female counterpart in relationship to Rebekah. Nonetheless, Rebekah suffered from sterility for twenty years. Finally, God hears the prayer of her husband Isaac and she gives birth to Jacob and Esau. (Genesis 25:19-26)

[13] Joseph Ratzinger, *Daughter Zion: Meditations on the Church's Marian Belief*, trans. McDermott (San Francisco: Ignatius Press, 1983), 18.

Jael, Esther and Judith. The prophetess Deborah along with the military commander Barak defeated the powerful Canaanite army led by Sisera. Jael killed Sisera by driving a tent peg into his forehead as he lay sleeping in her tent. (Judges 4:17-22) Esther successfully appealed to her king and husband Ahasuerus to put an end to the plot of Haman, a high ranking official, to kill the Jewish people. Judith cut off the head of the Assyrian Nebuchadnezzar's military commander Holofernes. She did so after entering his camp, enticing him with her beauty, getting him drunk and finally cutting off his head with his sword. Before doing so, she prayed, "For your strength does not depend on numbers, nor your might on the powerful. But you are the God of the lowly, helper of the oppressed, upholder of the weak, protector of the forsaken, savior of those without hope." (Judith 9:11 NRSV)

Women known for their power and influence also form part of the Old Testament theology of women. These women were called Queen Mothers. The role of the Queen Mother did not originate in Israel but rather from surrounding pagan societies, such as in Mesopotamia. These societies greatly honored their King's mother as a Queen mother. This is evident in the Epic of Gilgamesh in the character Ninsun, mother of Gilgamesh, king of Uruk.[14] Scott Hahn explains that since polygamy

---

[14] "The Epic of Gilgamesh," aina.org, http://www.aina.org/books/eog/eog.htm, (accessed May 12, 2016).

was practiced in ancient Near Eastern culture, it was difficult to determine who was the queen. Thus, arose the practice of recognizing the King's mother as queen.[15]

Beginning with Solomon's mother, Bathsheba, the Queen Mother played an important role in the Davidic kingdom. As Queen Mother, Bathsheba was second only to her son the king. She, consequently, gave advice to the king in a manner no one else could. She also represented the people's needs to the king as an intercessor.[16] The prominent advising and intercessory role of the Queen Mother is evident in 1 Kings 2:19-21. In this passage, after Bathsheba enters the court of her son, King Solomon, he rises out of respect for his mother. She then sits upon a throne to his right. Afterwards, she asks a favor from her son. Before she asks, Solomon promises he will not refuse her request. Affirming the influential role of the Queen Mother alongside her son the king, Jeremiah states, "Say to the king and to the queen mother, 'Come down from your thrones, for your glorious crowns will fall from your heads.'" (Jeremiah 13:18 NRSV) Similarly, 2 Kings 24:15 ranks the mother of the king directly after her son.[17]

---

[15] Scott Hahn, *Hail, Holy Queen* (New York: Image Books, 2001), 78.

[16] Matthew Leonard, *The Bible and the Virgin Mary Journey Through Scripture*, 5 DVDs (Steubenville: St. Paul Center for Biblical Theology, 2014).

[17] Matthew Leonard, *The Bible and the Virgin Mary Journey Through Scripture*, 5 DVDs (Steubenville: St. Paul Center for Biblical Theology, 2014).

Another prominent passage on the role of a Queen Mother is Proverbs 31. Proverbs 31 describes King Lemuel's Mother giving the king advice and reminding him to take care of the poor and those who have no one to speak for them. Interestingly, a Jewish tradition identifies King Lemuel with Solomon and, consequently, King Lemuel's mother with Bathsheba.[18]

The Woman from Genesis and Miriam

Two other women from the Old Testament who will factor into Old Testament theology of women are the woman described in Genesis 3:15 and Miriam, the sister of Moses. In Genesis 3:15 God promises that, "I will put enmity between you and the woman, and between your offspring and hers; he will crush your head, and you will strike his heel." (NRSV) Traditionally, this verse has been interpreted as signifying that Satan, represented by the serpent, will suffer a humiliating defeat by a woman and her child, the promised Messiah.[19]

Finally, we come to Miriam who in a way stands in a category of her own. As the sister of Moses she helped to guide the Israelites through their desert journey. Sadly, she failed in a number of ways. She

---

[18] Matthew Leonard, *The Bible and the Virgin Mary Journey Through Scripture*, 5 DVDs (Steubenville: St. Paul Center for Biblical Theology, 2014).

[19] Matthew Leonard, *The Bible and the Virgin Mary Journey Through Scripture*, Participant Workbook (Steubenville: St. Paul Center for Biblical Theology, 2014), 98.

did so by falling into idolatry and by challenging her brother as God's representative.[20] According to a Jewish tradition, though, despite her failings she provided for her people's needs during their desert journey. Her care is represented by the tradition of "Miriam's well" which Nissan Mindel describes as "a rolling rock that accompanied the Jewish people on their wanderings—provided fresh water in the desert, not only for the people but also for their cattle and sheep. It also made the desert bloom with green pastures and beautifully scented flowers."[21]

Daughter Zion

Besides honoring individual women, the Old Testament also greatly honors women in its theology by bestowing the title Daughter Zion on all of Israel.[22] As the prophet Zephaniah states, "Sing, Daughter Zion; shout aloud, Israel! Be glad and rejoice with all your heart, Daughter Jerusalem!" (Zephaniah 3:14 NRSV) Along with this feminine image and others, Israel is also portrayed as a

---

[20] Scott Hahn, *Hail, Holy Queen* (New York: Image Books, 2001), 72.

[21] Nissan Mindel, "Miriam," Chabad.org, http://www.chabad.org/library/article_cdo/aid/112396/jewish/Miriam.htm, (accessed May 24, 2016).

[22] A sampling of references of Israel as Daughter Zion include, 2 Kings 19:21, Psalm 9:14, Song of Solomon 3:11, Isaiah 1:8, Jeremiah 4:31, Lamentations 2:13, and Micah 1:13.

virgin[23] and as a bride.[24] These titles are typically treated within the over-arching biblical theme of Israel's covenantal marriage relationship with God. Since Israel is portrayed as married to God, infidelity to the covenant is described as adultery. The extended analogy of Israel's marriage to God is referred to by scripture scholars as an allegory which contains a number of analogies within one greater analogy. The Song of Songs is an example of an entire book that forms an extended allegory of marriage. Traditionally, both in Jewish traditions and Catholic tradition, the Song of Songs has been interpreted as not only a poem on human love but also a poem about the spiritual relationship of God as bridegroom and Israel as His bride.[25]

---

[23] Reference of Israel as virgin Israel include, Deuteronomy 22:19, Jeremiah 18:13, Jeremiah 31:4, Jeremiah 31:21, and Ezekiel 44:22.

[24] A sampling of references of Israel as bride include, 2 Samuel 17:3, Isaiah 49:18, Isaiah 61:10, Proverbs 2, Jeremiah 3, Ezekiel 16. In the last three references Israel's covenantal relationship with God is depicted as a marriage. Consequently, infidelity to the covenant is described as adultery. The extended analogy of Israel's marriage to God is referred to by scripture scholars as an allegory which contain a number of analogies within one greater analogy. Brant Pitre, *Jesus the Bridegroom: The Divine Love Story in the Bible,* Study Guide p. 13 and CD 4 (Catholic Productions). Pitre cites Raymond C. Ortlund *God's Unfaithful Wife: A Biblical Theology of Spiritual Adultery,* 83.

[25] Brant Pitre, *Jesus the Bridegroom: The Divine Love Story in the Bible,* Study Guide p. 16-17 and CD 4 (Catholic Productions). Pitre cites Ellen F. Davis's *Song of Songs.*

Discussion Questions

1. Distinguish the Old Testament theology of women from how women were incorporated in polytheistic theology. Include the following in your response: ritual intercourse, Aphrodite, God as Father, Aquinas's distinction between human fatherhood and the Fatherhood of God, and Genesis 1:27.

2. Choose one of the following infertile-fertile pairs of women: Sarah and Hagar, Rachel and Leah, and Hannah and Peninnah. Then, briefly describe the biblical account of these two women. Do so in relationship to blessings, fertility, and infertility.

3. Choose one of the following "powerless" women: Deborah, Jael, Esther and Judith. Then, briefly describe the biblical account of the woman you choose. Do so in respect to worldly power, Divine power, and the woman.

4. Explain the role of Queen Mother both in ancient Israel and outside of Israel. Include the following in your response: Epic of Gilgamesh, Bathsheba, King Lemuel, and the two principle roles of the Queen Mother.

5. Choose one of the following to respond to.

- The Song of Songs as an Allegory. Include in your response a brief description of the Song of Songs from both the perspective of human love and spiritual love. Finally, explain why it can be understood as an allegory.

- Genesis 3:15 with respect to the Messiah. Include in your response the verse, and an explanation of the characters in the verse.

- Miriam's role in relationship to the Israelites. Include in your response her role, Jewish tradition, and her failings.

Chapter 2

Foreshadowing in the Old Testament

Part II: Creation, Covenant, Abraham, Ark

Introduction

Pope Benedict XVI in a Wednesday Audience re-affirmed *Dei Verbum*'s explanation of how the Old Testament and the New Testament are related to one another. He said:

> After Mary, a pure reflection of the light of Christ, it is from the Apostles, through their word and witness, that we receive the truth of Christ. Their mission is not isolated, however, but is situated within a mystery of communion that involves the entire People of God and is carried out in stages from the Old to the New Covenant.
>
> In this regard, it must be said that the message of Jesus is completely misunderstood if it is separated from

the context of the faith and hope of the Chosen People: like John the Baptist, his direct Precursor, Jesus above all addresses Israel (cf. Mt 15:24) in order to "gather" it together in the eschatological time that arrived with him. And like that of John, the preaching of Jesus is at the same time a call of grace and a sign of contradiction and of justice for the entire People of God.

And so, from the first moment of his salvific activity, Jesus of Nazareth strives to gather together the People of God. Even if his preaching is always an appeal for personal conversion, in reality he continually aims to build the People of God whom he came to bring together, purify and save.[26]

Beginning with creation, in this chapter we will continue studying the Old Testament in order to better understand the faith and hope of God's Chosen People into whom Jesus was born by Mary.

---

[26] Benedict XVI, "Christ and the Church: The Pope Begins a New Series of Reflections on the Relationship Between Jesus and the Church in Light of the Apostles and the Duty They Received," March 15, 2006, ewtn.com, http://www.ewtn.com/library/PAPALDOC/b16ChrstChrch1.ht m, (accessed May 26, 2016).

The central role of covenant, Abraham's faith, and the ark will also be reflected upon in preparation for the following two chapters on Mary and the New Testament.

27

Creation

Genesis explicitly describes God as directly involved with physical matter. God is not presented as unconcerned and, even, incapable of relating to the physical world. Rather, He is described as directly involved with the physical world by creating it with time.[28] After creating the universe,

---

[27] Web Gallery of Art, "Eden (Lucas Cranach the Elder, 1472–1553)," photograph, https://commons.wikimedia.org/wiki/File%3AAdam_and_Eve_by_Lucas_Cranach_(I).jpg, (accessed June 26, 2016).

[28] Joseph Ratzinger, *Daughter Zion: Meditations on the Church's Marian Belief*, trans. McDermott (San Francisco:

God acknowledges that it is good and very good. This goodness of creation is presented in Genesis chapter one as reflecting the goodness of God. The fall of Adam and Eve that we read in chapter three is to be understood in light of the perfect goodness of God reflected in what he created and which will eventually triumph over evil. Hope in a future time when perfections of the creator will overcome evil are increasingly more clearly stated in the bible. This is especially the case in the prophetic litera-ture, such as in Daniel. Daniel describes a time when the apparent cyclical dimension of history, where one imperfect kingdom replaces another, will one day be definitively replaced by a fifth kingdom in which the perfections of creation that reflect the perfection of God its creator will triumph.[29]

The Old Testament scholar, Fr. Richard J. Clifford, S.J., explains that world history was understood in ancient times in reference to four kingdoms that endlessly succeeded one another. The specific identity of these kingdoms is of lesser importance than that there are four. The reason is that during ancient times the number four symbolized universality. For example, the expres-sion "four corners of the earth" was used to repre-sent the entire world. Similarly, a common ancient way that royal scribes described all of world history was by referring to four kingdoms that endlessly

---

Ignatius Press, 1983), 60; Frank Sheed, *Theology and Sanctity* (ebook: Catholic Way Publishing, 2014), loc. 1856.

[29] Fr. Richard J. Clifford, *Enjoying the Old Testament*, 9 CDs and Study Guide (Now You Know Media, 2013).

succeed each other. The identity of these kingdoms included the Assyrians, Babylonians, Medes, Persians, Greeks etc. Gods were understood as directly connected to these various kingdoms. As a god rose in prominence among other gods, his kingdom also rose and vice versa. According to Clifford, since the four-kingdom interpretation of world history was so common, it also was used in the bible but with a significant difference that is particularly evident in Daniel chapter seven (written c. 165 BC). In this chapter, a fifth kingdom, representing a renewed creation of God, is added to the four, thereby breaking the apparent endless cycle of sinful kingdoms. Daniel presents this fifth good Kingdom as an everlasting Kingdom.

Important aspects to note with respect to the Old Testament's account of creation is that God does interact with the physical world; God deeply cares for what he created; and the perfections of God reflected in his creation will one day in freedom triumph over sinful and imperfect aspects within creation.

Covenant

As thoroughly explained by Scott Hahn, the various covenants that God established with His Chosen People gradually prepare for the day when the traces and images of God's perfection in creation will triumph over the fallen and sinful aspects of creation.[30] While Ratzinger acknowledges, along with a consensus of scripture scholars, that the idea of covenant likely came from outside of Israel he also points out the unique way that the Israelites understood their covenant. Before seeing how the Israelite's concept of covenant differed from their neighbors, from whom they may have borrowed the idea, we will look at how a prominent Old Testament scholar, G.E. Mendenhall, first established a probable connection between Hittite suzerainty treaties and the covenant God established at the time of Moses.

G.E. Mendenhall was the first Old Testament scholar who persuasively argued that the covenant of the Ten Commandments is based on Hittite

---

[30] The following covenant chart is based on the following source. Sarah Christmyer, *A Quick Journey Through the Bible: An 8-Part Introduction to the Bible Timeline Student Workbook* (West Chester: Ascension Press, 2008), 12.

Family Form	Mediator	Covenant Sign
One Holy Couple	Adam (Gen 1-3)	Sabbath
One Holy Family	Noah (Gen 9)	Rainbow
One Holy Tribe	Abraham (Gen 15, 17,22)	Circumcision
One Holy Nation	Moses (Ex 24/ Deut 29)	Tablets
One Holy Kingdom	David/Solomon (II Sam. 7)	Ark and Tent/Temple
One Holy Catholic Church	Jesus (Mk 14)	Eucharist

suzerainty treaties. The Hittite suzerainty treaty was a type of international political treaty. In a Hittite suzerainty treaty:

> the vassal, consequent upon certain historical events enumerated in the prologue to the treaty, bound himself in absolute obedience to the Hittite king, but was left free to determine his state's internal affairs. While it was presupposed that the Hittite king would give to the vassal his protection, no specific obligations were laid upon him, and he was not a 'party' to the treaty.[31]

According to Mendenhall and other scholars, Yahweh fulfilled the role of the Hittite king and the Israelite people fulfilled the role of the vassal or state within the Hittite treaty. If these scholars are correct, then this historical influence indicates that this covenant is not to be understood as simply a legal code to keep order in society but rather is to be understood as a particular covenant between Yahweh the King and his vassal, the Israelite people. Moreover, as in the Hittite treaty, Yahweh is not considered as a party in the treaty, for then the covenant would only be a contractual agreement between two equal parties. Rather, seen

---

[31] Anthony Phillips, *Ancient Israel's Criminal Law* (New York: Schocken Books, 1970) 3.

in the light of the Hittite treaty, Yahweh, as depicted in Exodus, is a king who is granting a particular favored status to his vassals, the Israelite people, who are to honor certain obligations.[32]

What is being emphasized in this covenant, therefore, is the vertical relationship between Yahweh and the Israelites and not the horizontal relationships among the Israelites themselves. Whether one agrees with Mendenhall's thesis or not, what most can agree on is that the original, historical meaning of the Sinai covenant differs from our modern understanding of legal codes and reasons for punishing violators of a legal code. Ordinarily, we punish criminals in order to deter the criminal and others from breaking the law another time and as a just retribution for the crime committed. However, as Anthony Phillips points out, the reason Israel executed violators of the law was not "to deter potential criminals, nor as an act of retribution, but as a means of preventing divine action by appeasing Yahweh's wrath."[33] This is evident in Deuteronomy 21 which explains the reason for capital punishment as "a plea by the community that no divine action might be taken against them"[34] because of the violation of the covenant by one of their members.

---

[32] Anthony Phillips, *Ancient Israel's Criminal Law* (New York: Schocken Books, 1970) 3-4.

[33] Anthony Phillips, *Ancient Israel's Criminal Law* (New York: Schocken Books, 1970) 12.

[34] Anthony Phillips, *Ancient Israel's Criminal Law* (New York: Schocken Books, 1970) 11.

As was previously stated, Ratzinger acknowledges the reasonableness of Mendenhall's and
many other scripture scholars' argument that the
Old Testament idea of covenant was "probably ... at
first largely patterned after the model of ancient
Eastern vassal indentures, in which the sovereign
king assigns rights and duties."[35] This historical
origin, though, is insufficient to properly understand the covenantal relationship of God with
Israel. The reason is that, explains Ratzinger, the
"political and legal notion of the covenant, [were] ...
continually deepened and surpassed in the theology
of the prophets: the covenant relation of Yahweh to
Israel is a covenant of marital love, which—as in
Hosea's magnificent vision—moves and stirs
Yahweh himself to his heart."[36]

The uniqueness of how Israel began to
understand the covenantal relationship with God
was that, through revelation especially revelation
through the prophets, the relationship between
Israel and God was understood as a marriage covenant. This is related to how the Israelites distinguished their theology of women from the theology
of women of their neighbors. As we saw earlier,
surrounding polytheistic religions included women
in their theology by describing their god married to

---

[35] Joseph Ratzinger, *Daughter Zion: Meditations on the
Church's Marian Belief*, trans. McDermott (San Francisco:
Ignatius Press, 1983), 21-22.

[36] Joseph Ratzinger, *Daughter Zion: Meditations on the
Church's Marian Belief*, trans. McDermott (San Francisco:
Ignatius Press, 1983), 21-22.

a goddess. In contrast, the Israelites incorporated women in their theology by believing that the true God is married not to a Goddess but rather to the created reality of Israel who is called God's bride and spouse.[37] Understanding the marital aspect of the Israelite covenant, where Israel is portrayed as a created woman, is crucial since, argues Ratzinger, "to leave woman out of the whole of theology would be to deny creation and election (salvation history) and thereby to nullify revelation."[38]

Abraham's Faith

God's covenantal, marital relationship with Israel as a tribe of people began with Abraham's faith. This covenant was anticipated by the covenant God established with Adam and Eve as a married couple (Genesis 1-3) and with Noah and his family (Genesis 9). According to a Jewish tradition, Seven Noahide Commandments were given to Adam on the day when he was created.[39] These Noahide commandments were intended for all people, the tradition states. Since Adam and Eve's descendants broke these laws, God sent a great

---

[37] A sampling of references to Israel as bride and spouse are as follows. Ezekiel 23, 16; Isaiah 54:5, 62:5; Jeremiah 2:2, 3:14, Jeremiah 3:6-10, 13:27, Hosea 1:2, 2:4.

[38] Ratzinger, J. (1983). *Daughter Zion: Meditations on the Church's Marian Belief.* (J. M. McDermott, Trans.) (pp. 23–24). San Francisco: Ignatius Press.

[39] Chaim Clorfene, Yakov Rogalsky, *The Path of the Righteous Gentile: An Introduction to the Seven Laws of the Children of Noah* (Southfield: Targum Press, 1987), 4.

flood to purify the human race. The seven laws the descendants of Adam and Eve broke are as follows.

- Not to worship idols.
- Not to curse God.
- Not to kill [murder].
- Not to steal.
- Not to engage in sexual immorality.
- Not to eat the limb of a living animal.
- To establish courts of law to enforce these laws.[40]

According to the Letter to the Hebrews, faith is what connects Noah (and the Seven Noahide Commandments) with Israel's patriarch Abraham (Genesis 12):

> By faith Noah, when warned about things not yet seen, in holy fear built an ark to save his family. By his faith he condemned the world and became heir of the righteousness that is in keeping with faith.
>
> By faith Abraham, when called to go to a place he would later receive as his inheritance, obeyed and went, even though he did not know where he was going. By faith he made his

---

[40] Chaim Clorfene, Yakov Rogalsky, *The Path of the Righteous Gentile: An Introduction to the Seven Laws of the Children of Noah* (Southfield: Targum Press, 1987), 8.

home in the promised land like a
stranger in a foreign country; he
lived in tents, as did Isaac and Jacob,
who were heirs with him of the same
promise. For he was looking forward
to the city with foundations, whose
architect and builder is God. And by
faith even Sarah, who was past
childbearing age, was enabled to
bear children because she
considered him faithful who had
made the promise. And so from this
one man, and he as good as dead,
came descendants as numerous as
the stars in the sky and as countless
as the sand on the seashore.
(Hebrews 11: 7-12 NRSV)

Abraham's son, Isaac, was Israel's second
patriarch. He in turn was succeeded by his son
Jacob, who was Israel's third patriarch. (Genesis
35:12) Israel's name comes from the third
patriarch, Jacob, when God changed Jacob's name
to Israel after Jacob wrestled with an angel.
(Genesis 32:28-29 and 35:10) Jacob's, or Israel's,
twelve sons became the fathers of the Twelve Tribes
of Israel, which under Moses' leadership were
formed into a nation with the Ten Commandments
as their legal foundation and covenant with God.

Ark

For safe keeping and out of reverence for God's word and presence, the Ten Commandments, along with other items, were placed in a special container called the Ark of the Covenant. (Exodus 25:22 NRSV) According to Hebrews the Ark of the Covenant contained the Ten Commandments, an urn of manna, and the staff of Aaron:[41]

> Now even the first covenant had regulations for worship and an earthly sanctuary. For a tent was constructed, the first one, in which were the lampstand, the table, and the bread of the Presence; this is called the Holy Place. Behind the second curtain was a tent called the Holy of Holies. In it stood the golden altar of incense and the ark of the covenant overlaid on all sides with gold, in which there were a golden urn holding the manna, and Aaron's rod that budded, and the tablets of the covenant; above it were the cherubim of glory overshadowing the mercy seat. Of these things we cannot speak now in detail. (Hebrews 9:1-5 NRSV Cf. Exodus

---

[41] Cf Exodus 25:10-22; Brant Pitre, *Jesus and the Jewish Roots of the Eucharist* (New York: Doubleday, 2011), 33.

16:33-34, Numbers 17: 23, 25)

In Exodus chapter thirty-one, God reveals his laws to Moses by writing them on two stone tablets with His finger. (Exodus 31:18) These words of God written on stone both were the means by which God was intimately present to his people and gave the Israelites a specific way to follow in order to relate to God properly.

Exodus chapter sixteen identifies the jar of manna as a small portion of the "bread of from heaven" that God rained down upon the Israelites when they journeyed through the desert to the Promised Land. Interestingly, according to a Jewish oral tradition, this bread was with God from the beginning of creation. God kept it in reserve for times when the His Chosen People were in need of it.[42] As long as the Ark was with the Israelites, it was considered the center of God's presence on earth. (Numbers 10:33-36)

In numbers chapter seventeen, God miracu-

---

[42] According to the Mishnah the manna was one of the ten things that was created on the eve of the seventh day. Mishhah, Aboth 5 look up reference; 2 Baruch 29:3, 6-8. "3 And it shall come to pass when all is accomplished that was to come to pass in those parts, that the Messiah shall then begin to be revealed. ...8 And it shall come to pass at that self-same time that the treasury of manna shall again descend from on high, and they will eat of it in those years, because these are they who have come to the consummation of time." Cf. Brant Pitre Jesus and the Jewish Roots of the Eucharist 86-91.

lously causes Aaron's rod[43] to sprout, bud and produce "ripe almonds" in order to affirm that Aaron's Levite tribe were chosen to be His priests. (Numbers 17:8 NRSV) The rod, signifying priesthood, the jar of manna, signifying God's providential care, and the Ten Commandments, signifying God's presence, were all placed in the Ark of the Covenant.

Due to the Ark's role of being the epicenter of God's presence it was so sacred that a person could die if the ark was touched. This is what occurred to Uzzah after he touched the ark in order to steady it as it was being hauled by a team of oxen. (2 Samuel 6:6-7) To further signify the holiness of the Ark, the wood of the ark was acacia (Exodus 25:10). According to first-century AD Jewish historian Josephus, this wood was "naturally strong and could not be corrupted."[44]

Sadly, the Ark disappeared during the time of the Babylonian conquest of Southern Kingdom of Judah (c. 586 BC). The Second Book of the Maccabees informs us that the Ark was lost after Jeremiah hid it in a cave. (2 Macc. 2: 5-6) According to Jeremiah, the location of the ark will "remain unknown until God gathers his people together again and shows his mercy." (2 Macc. 2:7

---

[43] The rod that once changed into a snake that swallowed up the serpent-rods of Pharaoh's priests (Exodus 7:12),

[44] Flavius Josephus, "The Antiquities of the Jews", bk. 3, chap. 6, trans. William Whiston, gutenberg.org, http://www.gutenberg.org/files/2848/2848-h/2848-h.htm#link32HCH0006, (accessed May 27, 2016).

NRSV)[45]

Discussion Questions

1. In light of Pope Benedict XVI's Wednesday Audience, located online at http://www.ewtn.com/library/PAPALD OC/b16ChrstChrch1.htm entitled "Christ and the Church" printed in the L'Osservatore Romano March 22nd, 2006, discuss why the Catholic Church is new but not completely brand new since it is in continuity with what came before. Include in your response the following: Israel, Mary, the Apostles, Jesus, and the Church.

2. Discuss how the five kingdoms to which the prophet Daniel refers in chapter seven are an indication that one day the perfect goodness of God reflected in his creation will be victorious. Include in your response the following: Genesis chapter one and three, a pagan understanding of the four kingdoms, and Daniel's concept of the four kingdoms.

3. Even though Israel may have been influenced by their neighbor's understanding of a covenant, specifically the Hittite suzerainty treaty, explain how Israel's understanding of covenant differs from their neighbors'. Include in your answer the following: Hittite

---

[45] Brant Pitre, *Jesus and the Jewish Roots of the Eucharist* (New York: Doubleday, 2011), 33.

suzerainty treaty, Hosea, marriage, the Old Testament theology of women.

4. With specific reference to the Old Testament, compare and contrast Noah's faith with Abraham's faith. Include in your answer the following: The Seven Noahide Commandments, the Ten Commandments, Noah's faith, Abraham's faith.

5. Discuss the significance of the Ark of the Covenant, its three items, and the meaning of its disappearance.

Chapter 3

Fulfillment in the New Testament

Part I: Theology of Women

Introduction

The Old Testament theology of women was fulfilled in the New Testament theology of women as personified in Mary. In this chapter, we will see how Mary fulfills women and feminine aspects of the Old Testament in four ways: Mary as New Eve, Mary as the Woman of the Protoevangelium, Mary as Queen Mother, and Mary as Daughter Zion. Before doing so, though, we will first briefly look at key terminology that is used when explaining that the Old Testament is fulfilled in the New Testament and the New Testament is foreshadowed in the Old Testament.

Typology and Allegory

The words typology and allegory are often used to relate the Old Testament with the New Testa-ment. Typology is based on the Greek word *typos*, which means "a blow, dent, impression, or mark."[46] We use the base of this Greek word in typewriter, since typewriters make an impression by hitting paper with a metal hammer. According to a Catholic application of typology to the New Testament, types are in the Old Testament and antitypes, or the fulfilment of the types, are in the New Testament.

47

The most important antitype is Christ who fulfills the role of David, as a leader, Moses, as a law giver,

---

[46] "Type," Online Etymology Dictionary, http://www.etymonline.com/index.php?term=type, (accessed September 20, 2015).

[47]

http://freechristimages.org/biblestories/annunciation.htm, "F ulfiFu, 1898, Philadelphia Museum of Art," photograph, https://commons.wikimedia.org/wiki/File%3AHenry_Ossawa _Tanner_-_The_Annunciation.jpg, (accessed June 26, 2016).

Elijah, as a prophet, Melchizedek and Aaron, as a priest, etc. This does not mean, though, that typology is not present within the Old Testament itself. It is. In his book *Allegory and Event*, Richard Hanson demonstrates that ancient Jewish Rabbis "conceived of Israel's redemption in the Messianic Age as foreshadowed in every detail by the redemption from Egypt as its type. ... As Israel was fed with rich food in the Wilderness, so will God feed them at the Last time."[48]

If we now apply this way of interpreting the relationship to the Old Testament to the New Testament we may conclude the following. Once the types of the Old Testament are typed on the page of the New Testament they assume greater meaning since the page, representing the Word of Christ, brings all types into their fullest relationship with one another.[49]

A related term to typology is allegory. Allegory comes from a Greek word that literally means "a speaking about something else" from *allos* "meaning another" and *agoreuein* meaning to "speak in the assembly."[50] Unlike typology that

---

[48] Richard Patrick Crosland Hanson, *Allegory & Event: A Study of the Sources and Significance of Origin's Interpretation of Scripture*, (Louisville: Westminster John Knox Press, 2002), 13.

[49] Phillip Cary, *The History of Christian Theology* Lectures 1-18 (Chantilly: The Great Courses, 2008), 117.

[50] "Allegory," Online Etymology Dictionary, http://www.etymonline.com/index.php?allowed_in_frame=0

relates people and events horizontally through time, allegory, when it was first used, relates historical events vertically with trans-historical or spiritual realities.[51] For example, both in Jewish and in Christian tradition, the Song of Songs has been interpreted in an allegorical manner in which the human love portrayed in the poetry is vertically signifying the spiritual love between God and his Chosen People.

Beginning with Origin, Phillip Cary explains, the horizontal dimension of typology became assumed under the vertical dimension of allegory because Christ, by becoming incarnate, experienced time through his human nature, while transcending time as a divine person.[52] For this reason, in Christianity, the vertical allegorical reference to the Second Person of the Trinity arches over all types and is integrated with them.

In a way always subordinate to Christ's over-arching allegorical dimension, Marian types abound throughout the Old Testament. In the previous chapters, we covered a variety of specific women who are Marian types. These women include, but are not limited to, Eve, the Woman of Genesis, Queen Mother, and Daughter Zion.[53]

&search=allegory&searchmode=none, (accessed September 20, 2015).

[51] Phillip Cary, *The History of Christian Theology* Lectures 1-18 (Chantilly: The Great Courses, 2008), 122.

[52] Phillip Cary, *The History of Christian Theology* Lectures 1-18 (Chantilly: The Great Courses, 2008), 122.

[53] Scott Hahn, *Hail, Holy Queen* (New York: Image Books, 2001), 72.

Mary as New Eve

The name Eve comes from the Hebrew word *Hawwah* means "a living being."[54] The first Eve received her name because as Genesis chapter three explains, "The man named his wife Eve, because she was the mother of all living." (Genesis 3:20 NRSV) Interestingly, Ratzinger points out, Eve received her name after the Fall and not before. The reason for this, speculates Ratzinger, was to affirm that the "dignity and majesty of women"[55] remained after the Fall of Adam and Eve. This original feminine dignity and majesty of women due to the first woman's and all other women's relationship to life has been marred by women being, at times, a temptation for men.[56]

By being perfectly obedient to God, Mary became the new mother of the living who restores life, through her son Jesus, to mankind. We will see in a later chapter how early Church Fathers emphasized Mary's obedience. In summarizing this understanding of Mary's obedience in salvation history, Tim Staples, alluding to Scripture and to

---

[54] "Eve," etymonline.com, http://etymonline.com/index.php?allowed_in_frame=0&search=eve (accessed May 29, 2016).

[55] Joseph Ratzinger, *Daughter Zion: Meditations on the Church's Marian Belief*, trans. J.M. McDermott (San Francisco: Ignatius Press, 1983), 16.

[56] Joseph Ratzinger, *Daughter Zion: Meditations on the Church's Marian Belief*, trans. J.M. McDermott (San Francisco: Ignatius Press, 1983), 16.

commentary of the Church Fathers, states that while the Old Eve "reached out in disobedience to the tree of knowledge of good and evil and brought death to her children. Mary reaches out in faith to the tree of salvation, uniting with her son who brings eternal life."[57]

Mary as Woman of Genesis

The protoevangelium (protogospel) from Genesis 3:15 was touched upon previously. According to Catholic tradition, the promised Messiah who this verse assures will come to defeat Satan is Jesus Christ. Similarly, the woman of Genesis is Mary, the Mother of Jesus. Their victory, though, points out Saint Pope John Paul II in *Redemptoris Mater*, "will not take place without a hard struggle, a struggle that is to extend through the whole of human history."[58] God could have chosen an easier way to victory but, as St. Augustine asserts, "God created us without us: but he did not will to save us without us."[59] He will not

---

[57] Tim Staples, *Behold Your Mother: A Biblical and Historical Defense of the Marian Doctrines* (El Cajon: Catholic Answers, 2014), 104.

[58] John Paul II, "Redemptoris Mater," no. 11, w2.vatican.va, http://w2.vatican.va/content/john-paul-ii/en/encyclicals/documents/hf_jp-ii_enc_25031987_redemptoris-mater.html, (accessed May 29, 2016).

[59] "Catechism of the Catholic Church," no. 1847, Vatican.va, http://www.vatican.va/archive/ccc_css/archive/catechism/p3s1c1a8.htm, (accessed May 29, 2016). The

save us without us since He respects our free will and wants us to love Him freely. Mary as Mother of the Redeemer who will defeat Satan is, further explains the Holy Father,

> placed at the very center of that enmity, that struggle which accompanies the history of humanity on earth and the history of salvation itself. In this central place, she who belongs to the "weak and poor of the Lord" bears in herself, like no other member of the human race, that "glory of grace" which the Father "has bestowed on us in his beloved Son," and this grace determines the extraordinary greatness and beauty of her whole being. Mary thus remains before God, and also before the whole of humanity, as the unchangeable and inviolable sign of God's election, spoken of in Paul's letter: "in Christ...he chose us... before the foundation of the world...he destined us...to be his sons" (Eph. 1:4, 5). This election is more powerful than any experience of evil and sin, than all that "enmity" which marks the history of man. In

---

Catechism gives the following reference. St. Augustine, *Sermo* 169,11,13:PL 38,923.

this history Mary remains a sign of sure hope.[60]

Mary as Queen Mother

In his doctoral dissertation *Queen Mother: A Biblical Theology of Mary's Queenship*, Edward Sri carefully examines how Mary fulfills the Old Testament office of Queen Mother that we examined earlier. In his dissertation, Sri explains that the connection between the Old Testament Queen Mothers and Mary as a Queen Mother was examined with greater clarity after Vatican II, when:

> many scholars addressing this topic have taken a salvation-historical approach, using the Old Testament queen-mother tradition as the primary backdrop for understanding Mary's queenship.
>
> ...
>
> These scholars conclude that, with this Old Testament background in mind, Mary should be understood as the queen mother in the new kingdom of her Son. For example, in

---

[60] John Paul II, "Redemptoris Mater," no. 11, w2.vatican.va, http://w2.vatican.va/content/john-paul-ii/en/encyclicals/documents/hf_jp-ii_enc_25031987_redemptoris-mater.html, (accessed May 29, 2016).

the New Testament, Mary and Jesus are shown fulfilling Isaiah 7:14 (Mt. 1:22-3; Lk 1-26-31), thus connecting Mary with the queen-mother concept. Most of these scholars also point out how Mary is queen mother by returning to the Visitation scene, where Elizabeth calls Mary, "the mother of my Lord" - words probably used in reference to the queen mother in the Old Testament.[61]

As Queen Mother, Mary also intercedes to her son on behalf of her people, who comprise the Church. In heaven her intercessory role, evident at the Wedding of Cana (John 2:1-11), has been intensified and not eliminated. It would not make sense for God to grant her the role of intercessor to her son while on earth only to take this away from her in heaven. Antoine Nachef pointedly argues this point, by asserting:

What would persons be if, after living an entire life dedicated to God, they would lose their identity and

---

[61] Edward Sri, *Queen Mother A Biblical Theology of Mary's Queenship* (Steubenville: Emmaus Road Publishing, 2005), 37-38. Sri refers to the following scholars: H. Cazelles, A. Del Moral, D. Stanley, B. Ahern, C. Struhmueller and R. Laurentin.

> not remain themselves in heaven? ...
> Both the being and the action of the
> human person are perfected in
> heaven; otherwise there would be a
> lack of sincerity on the part of God
> who promised to give glory accord-
> ing to the degree of perfection that a
> person reaches in this life.[62]

The promise of God in Revelation that Nachef likely had in mind is from Matthew chapter sixteen, verse twenty-seven "For the Son of Man is to come with his angels in the glory of his Father, and then he will repay everyone for what has been done. (NRSV) In Romans chapter two, we also read, "For he will repay according to each one's deeds: to those who by patiently doing good seek for glory and honor and immortality, he will give eternal life; while for those who are self-seeking and who obey not the truth but wickedness, there will be wrath and fury." (Romans 2:6-8 NRSV) Similarly, Galatians chapter six, verse eight states, "If you sow to your own flesh, you will reap corruption from the flesh; but if you sow to the Spirit, you will reap eternal life from the Spirit." (NRSV)[63]

According to the dogmatic teaching of the Council of Florence, these and other similar Scripture passages teach that:

---

[62] Antoine Nachef, *Mary's Pope: John Paul II, Mary, and the Church Since Vatican II* (Franklin: Sheed & Ward, 2000), 151.

[63] Also see 1 Cor. 3:8, and 2 Cor. 9, 6.

> [T]he souls of those who have incurred no stain of sin whatsoever after baptism, as well as souls who after incurring the stain of sin have been cleansed whether in their bodies or outside their bodies, as was stated above, are straightaway received into heaven and clearly behold the triune God as he is, yet one person more perfectly than another according to the difference of their merits. But the souls of those who depart this life in actual mortal sin, or in original sin alone, go down straightaway to hell to be punished, but with unequal pains.[64]

Similarly, the Council of Trent teaches in canon 32 concerning justification:

> If anyone says that the good works of the one justified are in such manner the gifts of God that they are not also the good merits of him justified; or that the one justified by the good works that he performs by the grace of God and the merit of Jesus Christ,

---

[64] "Ecumenical Council of Florence (1438-1445)," Session 6 – 6 July 1439, ewtn.com, http://www.ewtn.com/library/COUNCILS/FLORENCE.HTM (accessed May 29, 2016).

whose living member he is, does not truly merit an increase of grace, eternal life, and in case he dies in grace, the attainment of eternal life itself and also an increase of glory, let him be anathema.[65]

Nachef states these doctrinal teachings from the Council of Florence and Trent in more contemporary language by writing, "Heaven becomes the radicalization and the ultimate perfection and realization of a person's being and action on earth."[66] Mary's maternal intercession while she was on earth as a fulfillment of the Old Testament role of Queen Mother, has, consequently, intensified in heaven in her role as Queen Mother of heaven and earth.

Mary as Daughter Zion

The final type that we will study is the personification of Israel as Daughter Zion. As was explained previously in reference to Ratzinger, the Old Testament incorporates women into its theology not by claiming that God is married to a Goddess, as pagan religions did, but rather by present-

---

[65] "The Council of Trent, Session VI – Celebrated on the thirteenth day of January, 1547 under Pope Paul III," ewtn.com, http://www.ewtn.com/library/COUNCILS/TRENT6.HTM, (accessed May 29, 2016).

[66] Antoine Nachef, *Mary's Pope: John Paul II, Mary, and the Church Since Vatican II* (Franklin: Sheed & Ward, 2000), 151.

ing the created, corporate reality of Israel as espoused to God. The title Daughter Zion was used in the Old Testament to signify this marital relationship between God and his Chosen People.[67]

For a detailed explanation from the Dominican Mark O'Brien on why the term Daughter Zion

---

[67] Mark O'Brien O.P., *Restoring the Right Relationship: The Bible on Divine Righteousness* (Hindmarsh: ATF Theology, 2014), 178. The Dominican Mark O'Brien summarizes the various citations in the Old Testament and explanations of the meaning of Daughter Zion as follows. The term Zion, especially in Isaiah, "is used variously to refer to the city/hill of Jerusalem (1:27; 2:3b; 4:3; 33:5, 20; 37:32; 20:9; 41:27, 52:1; 59:20;60:14; 62:1); the temple mount itself ... a combination of the city and temple mount ...; the seat of the Davidic king ... and God's house/dwelling place .... Zion is also described on a number of occasions as 'daughter Zion or 'daughter of Zion' (`1:8; 10:32; 16:1, 37:22, 52:2, 62:11). This combination exploits the feminine gender of the Hebrew word for city. Zion appears in later passages of the book as a mother bereft of her children but assured that they will return ..., as well as God's spouse (54:5-8). ... Given these passages are in Second- and Third-Isaiah this imagery may be an example of the creative use of the marriage metaphor from the earlier prophet Hosea. There it refers to the relationship between God and the holy city. One text even identifies Zion with the people (51:16b). Another image of Zion as a female figure is that of a 'whore' in 1:21. The term normally refers to a sexually unfaithful wife, daughter, or daughter-in-law. It could be portraying Zion as an unfaithful daughter, which would link it to references to 'daughter Zion,' but the context suggests the image of unfaithful wife is more likely, which would link it to the image of Zion as wife/mother in passages such as 54:5-8 and 62:1-5. In combination with the plural form 'daughters,' Zion forms a construct chain to refer to the female inhabitants of the city in 3:16 and 4:4."

signifies the spousal relationship between God and Israel, carefully read the corresponding footnote. O'Brien explains that Zion was used to refer to various aspect of the city of Jerusalem. Since the Hebrew word for city, *qiryah*, is feminine[68] it was referred to with a feminine title, Daughter Zion. This term, Daughter Zion, was understood as personifying the entire city of Jerusalem, representing God's Chosen People. In prophetic literature, in particular Hosea, the relationship between the Chosen People and God is described in nuptial terms. Hence, the relationship between Daughter Zion, personifying the Chosen People, and God was nuptially understood.

This Old Testament nuptial mystery, writes Ratzinger, "acquires its definitive meaning for the first time in the New Testament: in the woman who is herself described as the true holy remnant, as the authentic daughter Zion, and who is thereby the mother of the savior, yes, the mother of God."[69] In a similar way as the Daughter Zion represents all the People of Israel, Mary personifies the people of the Church. For this reason, *Lumen Gentium* of Vatican II names Mary the "Exalted Daughter of Zion."[70]

---

[68] Strong's Concordance, "7151.qiryah," biblehub.com, http://biblehub.com/hebrew/7151.htm, (accessed May 29, 2016).

[69] Joseph Ratzinger, *Daughter Zion: Meditations on the Church's Marian Belief*, trans. McDermott (San Francisco: Ignatius Press, 1983), 23-24.

[70] "Lumen Gentium," no. 55, Vatican.va, http://www.vatican.va/archive/hist_councils/ii_vatican_coun

St. John Paul II explains the difference between the Daughter of Zion of old and the Daughter of Zion who is Mary by saying, "With Mary, 'daughter of Zion' is not merely a collective subject, but a person who represents humanity and, at the moment of the Annunciation, she responds to the proposal of divine love with her own spousal love. Thus, she welcomes in a quite special way the joy foretold by the prophecies, a joy which reaches its peak here in the fulfilment of God's plan."[71] Unlike the Old Testament Zion who was a collective subject of the people of Israel, Mary personifies in her very person humanity's spousal relationship to God.

In relating Mary's spousal relationship with God to her title Daughter Zion, St. John Paul II asserts, "As the new 'daughter of Zion', Mary represents all humanity, called to the marriage banquet which celebrates God's Covenant with his people."[72] In accordance with this spousal imagery, the *Catechism of the Catholic Church* likewise

cil/documents/vat-ii_const_19641121_lumen-gentium_en.html, (accessed May 29, 2016).

[71] John Paul II, "Mary Responds to God with Spousal Love," no. 5, ewtn.com, https://www.ewtn.com/library/PAPALDOC/JP2BVM18.HTM, (accessed May 29, 2016). The following source is cited. L'Osservatore Romano Weekly Edition in English May 8, 1996, page 11.

[72] John Paul II, "Mary Responds to God with Spousal Love," no. 5, ewtn.com, https://www.ewtn.com/library/PAPALDOC/JP2BVM18.HTM (accessed May 29, 2016). The following source is cited. L'Osservatore Romano Weekly Edition in English May 8, 1996, page 11.

states that our fundamental spousal vocation to God is fulfilled in Mary. "The spousal character of the human vocation in relation to God is fulfilled perfectly in Mary's virginal motherhood."[73] It is fulfilled perfectly as the New Daughter Zion.

Discussion Questions

1. Discuss in reference to typology how the Old Testament foreshadows the New Testament. Include in your response the following: etymology of the word typology, typology in the Old Testament without relationship to the New Testament, typology within the Old Testament in relationship to the New Testament, the Christian transformation of typology and allegory.

2. Compare and contrast the Eve of the Old Testament with the New Eve of the New Testament. Include in your response the dignity of women and obedience with respect to both Eve and Mary.

3. Discuss how Mary and Jesus fulfill Genesis 3:15. Do so with specific reference to the verse. In addition, discuss, in reference to this verse, why St. John Paul II describes Mary as "a sign of sure hope."

4. Why is Mary considered Queen of Heaven and Earth? Include the following: Queen

---

[73] "Catechism of the Catholic Church," no. 505, Vatican.va, http://www.vatican.va/archive/ccc_css/archive/catechism/p1 22a3p2.htm, (accessed May 29, 2016).

Mother in the Old Testament, how Mary fulfilled this role while on earth (cite a specific New Testament passage), how Mary fulfills this role in heaven, and the Council of Trent.

5. Compare and Contrast the Old Testament Daughter of Zion with the New Testament Daughter of Zion. Include at least the following in your response: collective subject, spousal relationship.

Chapter 4

Fulfillment in the New Testament

Part II: New Creation, Mary's Faith, New Covenant, New Ark

Introduction

Not only persons of the Old Testament were fulfilled in the New Testament but also essential aspects of the Old Testament were fulfilled principally by Christ and, always in a subordinate sense, by Mary. The aspects that this chapter will focus on in relationship to Mary are as follows: creation, faith, covenant, and ark.

74

New Creation

As explained by Richard J. Clifford, the Old Testament presents creation in four ways: creation, fault, flood, and new creation.[74] The creation of the world is described in Genesis chapters one and two. The fault, or fall of Adam and Eve, is presented in chapter 3 which also in verses 15, within Christian tradition, foretells a new creation. The belief of a future new, or more accurately, renewed creation which will reflect without mar the perfection of its perfect creation is explicitly stated in chapter sixty-five of Isaiah:

> For I am about to create new heavens and a new earth; and the former things shall not be remembered or come to mind. And be glad and rejoice forever in what I am creating, for I am about to create Jerusalem as a joy, and its people as a delight. (Isaiah 65: 17-18 NRSV)

This new Jerusalem would also be a new Daughter Zion since, as was explained earlier, the term Daughter Zion is used in the Old Testament to personify Jerusalem. As explained in the previous chapter, Mary is the New Daughter Zion who personifies in her person a new people and a new creation. *Lumen Gentium* identifies Mary with the

[74] Fr. Richard J. Clifford, *Enjoying the Old Testament*, 9 CDs and Study Guide (Now You Know Media, 2013).

promised new creation by describing her as "fashioned by the Holy Spirit and formed as a new creature."[75] She is a new creature, preached Blessed John Henry Newman, because in her:

> I observe, that in her the curse pronounced on Eve was changed to a blessing. Eve was doomed to bear children in sorrow; but now this very dispensation, in which the token of Divine anger was conveyed, was made the means by which salvation came into the world. ... The very punishment of the fall, the very taint of birth-sin, admits of a cure by the coming of Christ.[76]

John Paul II further develops the theological presentation of Mary as a new creature, and even refers to her as a "new creation" because of Christ, by writing in *Mulieris Dignitatem* that:

> Eve, as "the mother of all the living"

---

[75] "Lumen Gentium," no. 56, Vatican.va, http://www.vatican.va/archive/hist_councils/ii_vatican_coun cil/documents/vat-ii_const_19641121_lumen-gentium_en.html, (accessed May 30, 2016).

[76] "Parochial and Plain Sermons, Volume 2, Sermon 12, The Reverence Due to the Virgin Mary," 127:1, newmanreader.org, http://www.newmanreader.org/works/parochial/volume2/ser mon12.html, (accessed May 30, 2016).

(Gen 3: 20), is the witness to the biblical "beginning", which contains the truth about the creation of man made in the image and likeness of God and the truth about original sin. Mary is the witness to the new "beginning" and the "new creation" (cf. 2 Cor 5:17), since she herself, as the first of the redeemed in salvation history, is "a new creation": she is "full of grace". ...

Mary, therefore, is a new creation because she was the first who was redeemed in an anticipatory manner by Christ. Consequently, she is without imperfection and full of grace. By creating Mary, John Paul II adds, God returns creation back "to that 'beginning' in which one finds the 'woman' as she was intended to be in creation, and therefore in the eternal mind of God: in the bosom of the Most Holy Trinity. Mary is "the new beginning" of the dignity and vocation of women, of each and every woman."[77]

For John Paul II, Mary is a new creation because she was untouched by sin, full of grace, is the New Eve as a restoration of creation, and gave

---

[77] John Paul II, "Mulieris Dignitatem," no. 11, w2.vatican.va, http://w2.vatican.va/content/john-paul-ii/en/apost_letters/1988/documents/hf_jp-ii_apl_19880815_mulieris-dignitatem.html, (accessed May 30, 2016).

birth to Christ, the New Adam.[78] It is proper to call Christ's assuming a human nature as well a new creation since, explains Ratzinger, "Jesus' conception and birth signify a new involvement in history that exceeds the uniqueness belonging to every single human being. At this point God himself begins anew. What begins here has the quality of a new creation, owing to God's own totally specific intervention."[79]

Mary's Faith

The Old Creation intertwined and knotted up by sin was disentangled by Mary's faith. Pope Francis in the celebration of the 2013 Year of Faith explained this ancient understanding of Mary that dates back to the Patristic age during his Address:

> The "knot" of disobedience, the "knot" of unbelief. When children disobey their parents, we can say that a little "knot" is created. ...

---

[78] Cf. "Lumen Gentium," no. 7, Vatican.va, http://www.vatican.va/archive/hist_councils/ii_vatican_coun cil/documents/vat-ii_const_19641121_lumen-gentium_en.html, (accessed May 30, 2016). "7. In the human nature united to Himself the Son of God, by overcoming death through His own death and resurrection, redeemed man and re-molded him into a new creation."

[79] Joseph Ratzinger, *Daughter Zion: Meditations on the Church's Marian Belief*, trans. McDermott (San Francisco: Ignatius Press, 1983), 47-48.

These knots take away our peace and serenity. They are dangerous, since many knots can form a tangle which gets more and more painful and difficult to undo.

But we know one thing: nothing is impossible for God's mercy! Even the most tangled knots are loosened by his grace. And Mary, whose "yes" opened the door for God to undo the knot of the ancient disobedience, is the Mother who patiently and lovingly brings us to God, so that he can untangle the knots of our soul by his fatherly mercy. ... She, as a woman of faith, will surely tell you: "Get up, go to the Lord: he understands you". And she leads us by the hand as a Mother, our Mother, to the embrace of our Father, the Father of mercies.[80]

With respect to the Old Testament, Mary's faith played a role similar to Abraham's faith in that both of their faiths began covenants. Abraham's faith

---

[80] Pope Francis, "Prayer for the Marian Day on the Occasion of the Year of Faith: Address of Holy Father Francis, Saint Peter's Square, 12 October 2013," no. 1, w2.vatican.va, http://w2.vatican.va/content/francesco/en/speeches/2013/october/documents/papa-francesco_20131012_preghiera-mariana.html, (accessed May 31, 2016).

began the Old Covenant between God and his Israelites, named after Abraham's grandson Jacob. When Mary believed and gave her yes to the Angel Gabriel, the New Covenant began. In comparing these two covenants from the perspective of faith, John Paul II writes in *Redemptoris Mater*:

> Mary's faith can also be compared to that of Abraham, whom St. Paul calls "our father in faith" (cf. Rom. 4:12). In the salvific economy of God's revelation, Abraham's faith constitutes the beginning of the Old Covenant; Mary's faith at the Annunciation inaugurates the New Covenant. Just as Abraham "in hope believed against hope, that he should become the father of many nations" (cf. Rom. 4:18), so Mary, at the Annunciation, having professed her virginity ("How shall this be, since I have no husband?") believed that through the power of the Most High, by the power of the Holy Spirit, she would become the Mother of God's Son in accordance with the angel's revelation: "The child to be born will be called holy, the Son of God" (Lk. 1:35).[81]

---

[81] John Paul, "Redemptoris Mater," no. 14, w2.vatican.va, http://w2.vatican.va/content/john-paul-

In commenting on John Paul II's Marian writings, Antoine Nachef points out that while being similar, the faith of Abraham differed significantly from the faith of Mary. This is evident when we compare the fulfillment of God's promise to Abraham that he "shall be the ancestor of a multitude of nations" (Genesis 17:4 NRSV) with the fulfillment of God's promise to Mary that "you will conceive in your womb and bear a son, and you will name him Jesus." (Luke 1: 31 NRSV) For Abraham, God fulfilled his promise through Abraham's wife, Sarah, by natural, human generation. However, in Mary's case, God fulfilled his promise not through natural, human generation but rather by the power of the Holy Spirit.[82]

New Covenant

What does John Paul II mean by stating that Mary "inaugurated the New Covenant"? Did not Jesus begin the New Covenant? After all, according to Hebrews, Jesus Christ "set aside the first to establish the second." (Hebrews 10:9 NRSV) This apparent difficulty is resolved when, as well explained by Tim Staples in a Thomistic manner, the

---

ii/en/encyclicals/documents/hf_jp-ii_enc_25031987_redemptoris-mater.html, (accessed May 31, 2016).

[82] Antoine Nachef, *Mary's Pope: John Paul II, Mary, and the Church Since Vatican II* (Franklin: Sheed & Ward, 2000), 121-122.

order of grace is distinguished from the order of time. "In the order of grace" Staples writes, "Jesus is the inaugurator, the source-indeed, Jesus Christ is the New Covenant. But in the order of time, as the grace of Christ is actually communicated to the world ... Mary was the first person to experience the redemption of Christ in her person. This grace, the grace of the New Covenant, was incarnate in Mary before the Incarnation [by her Immaculate Conception] – from the moment of her conception – and it was perfected in her through her declaration of faith and obedience."[83]

From the standpoint of time Mary's Immaculate Conception preceded the incarnation and provided the proper context in which the source of the New Covenant, Jesus, was born. In Mary, the New Covenant began as a new creation, untouched by sin, out of which came the most fitting environment for Jesus Christ, the New Adam and the New Covenant, to be born.[84] As a new creation preserved by sin by "the merits of Jesus Christ"[85] Mary, writes John Paul II, "utter[ed] the first fiat of the New

---

[83] Tim Staples, *Behold Your Mother: A Biblical and Historical Defense of the Marian Doctrines* (El Cajon: Catholic Answers, 2014), 77-78.

[84] Tim Staples, *Behold Your Mother: A Biblical and Historical Defense of the Marian Doctrines* (Kindle Edition, El Cajon: Catholic Answers, 2014), loc. 1201 of 6088.

[85] Pius IX, "Ineffabilis Deus, Apostolic Constitution Issued by Pope Pius IX on December 8, 1854," papalencyclicals.net, http://www.papalencyclicals.net/Pius09/p9ineff.htm, (accessed May 3, 2016).

Covenant."[86]

By providing the most fitting place for Jesus to be conceived, Mary also serves as a bridge between the Old Covenant and the New Covenant. The two are different, but not in the sense that there is no on-going relationship between the two. In describing how Mary links together in her person the two covenants Ratzinger writes, "As the holy remnant Mary signifies that in herself Old and New Covenants are really one. She is entirely a Jewess, a child of Israel, of the Old Covenant, and as such a child of the full covenant, entirely a Christian: Mother of the Word. She is the New Covenant in the Old Covenant; she is the New Covenant as the Old Covenant, as Israel."[87]

A key difference, which was pointed out previously, between the Old Covenant of the old creation and the New Covenant of the new creation is that unlike the unfertile women who foreshadowed Mary's miraculous birth of Jesus (Sarah, Rachel, Hannah, and even Elizabeth), in Mary's case, Joseph had a much less significant role since he was only the foster father of Jesus and not his biological, actual father. The actual father of Jesus is the Heavenly Father and not Joseph. In reference

---

[86] John Paul II, "Redemptoris Mater," no. 1, w2.vatican.va, http://w2.vatican.va/content/john-paul-ii/en/encyclicals/documents/hf_jp-ii_enc_25031987_redemptoris-mater.html, (accessed May 15, 2016).

[87] Joseph Ratzinger, *Daughter Zion: Meditations on the Church's Marian Belief*, trans. McDermott (San Francisco: Ignatius Press, 1983), 65.

to the Virgin Birth of Jesus, Hans Urs von Balthasar writes that "the decisive appearance of God as the sole Father ... excludes a relation to another father...."[88] In the New Covenant, therefore, further explains von Balthasar, "The whole process of bodily begetting, in fact, the whole question of whether a man or woman is fruitful or not, loses its importance."[89]

New Ark

Mary as the New Ark sheds light on why she may be called a New Creation and even be called the "inaugurator" of the New Covenant. As was explained previously, Mary is the "inaugurator" of the New Covenant from the perspective of time. In time, Mary as the "inaugurator" New Covenant and as the New Creation provided the perfect dwelling place for the source of the New Covenant who is Jesus. As the perfect dwelling place for Jesus, Mary is the perfect holy New Ark of the New Covenant. Her holiness comes not from herself but because of who dwelt within her, Jesus. Similarly, the Old Testament ark was not considered by the Israelites as holy by itself, but rather was considered holy because of what it housed, the Ten Command-

---

[88] Joseph Ratzinger, Hans Urs von Balthasar, trans. A. Walker *Mary: the Church at the Source* (San Francisco: Ignatius Press, 2005), 152.

[89] Joseph Ratzinger, Hans Urs von Balthasar, trans. A. Walker *Mary: the Church at the Source* (San Francisco: Ignatius Press, 2005), 152.

ments.[90]

One example of an early Father of the Church explicitly identifying Mary as a holy New Ark is St. Ambrose who wrote:

> The prophet David danced before the Ark. Now what else should we say the Ark was but holy Mary? The Ark bore within it the tables of the Testament, but Mary bore the Heir of the same Testament itself. The former contained in it the Law, the latter the Gospel. The one had the voice of God, the other His Word. The Ark, indeed, was radiant within and without with the glitter of gold, but holy Mary shone within and without with the splendor of virginity. The one was adorned with earthly gold, the other with heavenly.[91]

The holiness, and consequently, untouchability of the Old Ark is likewise fulfilled in Mary not in the sense that if someone touched her they would die, as happened with Uzzah when he touched the ark (2 Samuel 6:6-7), but rather by her being a per-

---

[90] Scott Hahn, *Hail, Holy Queen* (New York: Image Books, 2001), 60.

[91] Thomas Livius, *The Blessed Virgin in the Fathers of the First Six Centuries* (London: Burns and Oates, 1893), 77. The following source is cited. Serm. xlii. 6, Int. Opp., S. Ambrosii.

petual virgin and by being untouched by sin, two Marian doctrines we will study in another chapter. [92]

Discussion Questions

1. Discuss how Mary as a new creation. Do so in the context of creation, fault, flood, and new creation. Include the following in your response: Holy Spirit, curses, and new beginning both in reference to Christ and to Mary.

2. Compare and contrast Mary's faith with Abraham's faith. Include the following in your response: covenants, faith, obedience, and human and divine generation.

3. Discuss how Mary began the New Covenant and how Jesus began the New Covenant. Include the following in your response: order of time, order of grace, bridge, and difference from the Old Covenant with respect to birth and fatherhood.

4. Compare and contrast Mary as New Ark with the Old Testament Ark. Include the following in your response: incorruptibility, untouchability, Ten Commandments, and Jesus.

---

[92] Scott Hahn, *Hail, Holy Queen* (New York: Image Books, 2001), 104.

Chapter 5

Mary in the New Testament

Introduction

In this chapter, we will examine more closely how Mary fulfilled types in the Old Testament by studying specific passages from scripture. We will begin with New Testament accounts of the Annunciation, the Visitation, and the Wedding of Cana. This will be followed by Mary at Pentecost, and Mary's hidden presence in Revelation chapter eleven and twelve.

Annunciation

Compare Luke 1:28-37 with Zephaniah 3:14. According to Ratzinger, it is almost without dispute that the words the Angel Gabriel spoke to Mary, "take up the substance of the promise to daughter Zion in Zephaniah 3:14 that announces to her that God dwells in her midst."[93] Do you agree with this assessment?

---

[93] Joseph Ratzinger, Hans Urs von Balthasar, trans. A. Walker *Mary: the Church at the Source* (San Francisco: Ignatius Press, 2005), 88.

94

---

94 Unknown, "Eastern Christianity fresco of the Visitation in St. George Church in Kurbinovo, Macedonia," photograph, https://commons.wikimedia.org/wiki/File%3ATh e_Embrace_of_Elizabeth_and_the_Virgin_Mary.jpg, (accessed June 27, 2016).

Matthew Leonard, points out that the angel Gabriel's announcement in Luke 1 "Hail full of grace..." is "almost word for word"[95] from Zephaniah 3:14-18. (RSV) He also demonstrates that Luke's hail, at times translated as rejoice, "is the same word that Israel's prophets used to begin prophecies about the promised Messiah and the joy He would bring to God's people (Joel 2:23-24; Zech 9:9)."[96] I have placed similar verses in bold.

Luke 1:28-33 NRSV	Zephaniah 3:14-16 NRSV
28 And he came to her and said, **"Greetings, favored one!** The Lord is with you." ... 30 The angel said to her, **"Do not be afraid**, Mary, for you have found favor with God. 31 And now, **you will conceive in your womb and bear a son, and you will name him Jesus**. 32 He will be great, and will be called the Son of the Most High, and the Lord God will give to him	14 **Sing aloud, O daughter Zion**; shout, O Israel! Rejoice and exult with all your heart, O daughter Jerusalem! 15 The Lord has taken away the judgments against you, he has turned away your enemies. **The king of Israel, the Lord, is in your midst**; **you shall fear disaster no more**. 16 On that day it shall be said to Jerusalem: **Do not fear, O Zion**; do not let

---

95 Matthew Leonard, *The Bible and the Virgin Mary Journey Through Scripture*, Participant Workbook (Steubenville: St. Paul Center for Biblical Theology, 2014), 27.

96 Matthew Leonard, *The Bible and the Virgin Mary Journey Through Scripture*, Participant Workbook (Steubenville: St. Paul Center for Biblical Theology, 2014), 27.

the throne of his ancestor David. 33 He will reign over the house of Jacob forever, and of his kingdom there will be no end."	your hands grow weak.

With reference to the Angel Gabriel's words to Mary, Ratzinger adds that not only does the Angel Gabriel indicate in his greeting that Mary is the "daughter Zion in person," but also that she is "the place of God's inhabitation, the holy tent, upon which the cloud of God's presence rests."[97] Very likely the passages from the Old Testament that refer to a cloud that descends over the tabernacle containing the ark are the corresponding verses that Ratzinger has in mind. These include the following: Exodus 14:20, 40:34-38, Leviticus 9:23, 24; Numbers 9:15-23, 16:19. Below, the above mentioned passage from Exodus is placed side by side with the verses from Luke. In addition, Luke 1:36 has been placed aside Genesis 18:14 in order to compare Mary with Sarah. By drawing a compare-son between Mary and Sarah, writes Matthew Leonard, "Luke shows us that Mary, like Sarah, is being called to bear the Son of God's covenant promise. Those words also connect Mary to all the

[97] Joseph Ratzinger, Hans Urs von Balthasar, trans. A. Walker *Mary: the Church at the Source* (San Francisco: Ignatius Press, 2005), 88.

other miraculous births in salvation history."[98]

Luke 1:34-35 NRSV	Exodus 40:34-35 NRSV
34 Mary said to the angel, "How can this be, since I am a virgin?" 35 The angel said to her, "The **Holy Spirit will** come upon you, and the power of the Most High **will overshadow you**; therefore the child to be born will be holy; he will be called Son of God.	34 Then the **cloud covered the tent of meeting**, and the **glory of the Lord filled the tabernacle**. 35 Moses was not able to enter the tent of meeting because the cloud settled upon it, and the glory of the Lord filled the tabernacle.

Luke 1:36 NRSV	Genesis 18:13-14 NRSV
36 And now, your relative Elizabeth in her old age has also conceived a son; and this is the sixth month for her who was said to be barren. 37 **For nothing will be impossible with God**."	13 The Lord said to Abraham, "Why did Sarah laugh, and say, 'Shall I indeed bear a child, now that I am old?' 14 **Is anything too wonderful for the Lord**? At the set time I will return to you, in due season, and Sarah shall have a son."

Noticing the above-mentioned similarity between the overshadowing of the Holy Spirit over

---

[98] Matthew Leonard, *The Bible and the Virgin Mary Journey Through Scripture*, Participant Workbook (Steubenville: St. Paul Center for Biblical Theology, 2014), 28.

Mary and the cloud of God's glory over the Israelites holy tent containing the ark, the Fathers of the Church described Mary as the New Ark. This, explains Ratzinger:

> in turn had a decisive influence on ancient Christian iconography. Joseph is identified by the flowering staff as a high priest, as the prototype of the Christian bishop. For her part, Mary is the living Church. It is upon her that the Holy Spirit descends, thereby making her the new Temple. Joseph, the just man, is appointed to be the steward of the mysteries of God, the paterfamilias and guardian of the sanctuary, which is Mary the bride and the Logos in her. He thus becomes the icon of the bishop, to whom the bride is betrothed; she is not at his disposal but under his protection.[99]

Visitation

Luke's account of Mary's visitation to her cousin Elizabeth is often compared with two passages from the books of Samuel. The first selection relates to

---

[99] Joseph Ratzinger, Hans Urs von Balthasar, trans. A. Walker *Mary: the Church at the Source* (San Francisco: Ignatius Press, 2005), 88.

Luke 1:39-45, 56. The second relates to Luke 1:46-48. If we interpret Mary in the visitation as the New

100

Ark of the New Covenant whose origin is Jesus, then the following similarities may be made. First, Mary is visiting her cousin Elizabeth, who belongs

---

100 Flickr, "Joseph with the Child and the Flowering Rod, Alonso Miguel de Tovar (1678-1758)," photograph, https://commons.wikimedia.org/wiki/File%3ASan_Jos%C3%A9_-_Alonso_Miguel_de_Tovar.jpg, (accessed September 23, 2016).

to the priestly tribe of the Levites. Similarly, the ark of the Old Covenant is brought to house of Abinadab, whose son Eleazar was consecrated and placed in charge of the ark. (1 Samuel 7:1) [101]

As a member of the Levitical priestly tribe, Elizabeth praises Mary the New Ark. Her praise is joined by the praise of the son within her womb who leaps in joy.[102] Similarly, all of Israel along with King David, who dances and leaps, joyfully welcome the ark of the Old Covenant. In addition, Mary, the New Ark, and the ark of the Old Covenant both stay for three months at the place at which they arrive.

With respect to the three items in the ark of the Old Covenant (Ten Commandments as the Words from God written on stone, Manna as the heavenly bread, and the Priestly Rod of Aaron), Matthew Leonard shows how these are all fulfilled in Mary as the New Ark since Jesus is the Word of God (John 1:1), Jesus is the Manna (bread) from heaven (John 6:48-50), and Jesus is the true High Priest (Hebrews 4:14).[103]

---

[101] Scott Hahn, Catholic Bible Dictionary (New York: Doubleday, 2009), 9.

[102] Matthew Leonard, *The Bible and the Virgin Mary Journey Through Scripture*, 5 DVD series, (Steubenville: St. Paul Center for Biblical Theology, 2014).

[103] Matthew Leonard, *The Bible and the Virgin Mary Journey Through Scripture*, Participant Workbook (Steubenville: St. Paul Center for Biblical Theology, 2014), 58-59.

Luke 1:39-56 NRSV	2 Samuel 6:2-11 NRSV
39 In those days Mary set out and went with haste to a Judean town in the hill country, 40 where **she entered** the house of Zechariah and greeted Elizabeth. 41 When Elizabeth heard Mary's greeting, the **child leaped in her womb.** And Elizabeth was filled with the Holy Spirit 42 and exclaimed with a loud cry, "Blessed are you among women, and blessed is the fruit of your womb. 43 **And why has this happened to me, that the mother of my Lord comes to me?** 44 For as soon as I heard the sound of your greeting, the child in my womb leaped for joy. 45 And blessed is she who believed that there would be a fulfillment of what was spoken to her by the Lord." ... 56. **Mary stayed with Elizabeth for about three months** and then returned home.	2 David and all the people with him set out and went from Baale-judah, to bring up from there the ark of God, which is called by the name of the Lord of hosts who is enthroned on the cherubim. 3 They **carried the ark of God on a new cart**, and brought it out of the house of Abinadab, which was on the hill. Uzzah and Ahio, the sons of Abinadab, were driving the new cart 4 with the ark of God; and Ahio went in front of the ark. 5 **David and all the house of Israel were dancing before the Lord with all their might**, with songs and lyres and harps and tambourines and castanets and cymbals. ... 9 David was afraid of the Lord that day; he said, **"How can the ark of the Lord come into my care?"** 10 So David was unwilling to take the ark of the Lord into his care in the city of David; instead David took it to the house of

79

	Obed-edom the Gittite. **11 The ark of the Lord remained in the house of Obed-edom the Gittite three months**; and the Lord blessed Obed-edom and all his household.

The next two passages compare Mary with Hannah. They are similar in that Hannah was one of the infertile woman of the Old Testament infertile-fertile pairs of women (Sarah-Hagar, Rachel-Leah, and Hannah-Peninnah).[104] Due to God's intervention, Sarah, Rachel, Hannah, and Mary all are blessed with fertility. Mary differs from the other women in that she remained a virgin after the divine intervention. One reason for this difference is that Mary is the fulfillment of the previous women who only foreshadowed her role in

---

[104] Two other biblical women who were not paired with other women and despite their infertility were blessed by God so that they could give birth were the mother of Samson (Judges 13:2) and Elizabeth, mother of John the Baptist. "2 There was a certain man of Zorah, of the tribe of the Danites, whose name was Manoah. His wife was barren, having borne no children. 3 And the angel of the Lord appeared to the woman and said to her, "Although you are barren, having borne no children, you shall conceive and bear a son. 4 Now be careful not to drink wine or strong drink, or to eat anything unclean, 5 for you shall conceive and bear a son. No razor is to come on his head, for the boy shall be a nazirite to God from birth." Judges 13:2-5 NRSV)

salvation history as the Mother of God, and Mother of the Messiah.[105] If we look at the two textual comparisons given below, the similarities between Mary and Hannah are immediately apparent. Both refer to themselves as servants, or maidservants of the Lord, and both praise God in similar language.

Luke 1:46-48 NRSV	1 Samuel 1:9-11 NRSV
And Mary said, "My soul magnifies the Lord, 47 and my spirit rejoices in God my Savior, 48 for he has looked with favor on the lowliness of his **servant**. Surely, from now on all generations will call me blessed;	9 After they had eaten and drunk at Shiloh, Hannah rose and presented herself before the Lord. Now Eli the priest was sitting on the seat beside the doorpost of the temple of the Lord. 10 She was deeply distressed and prayed to the Lord, and wept bitterly. 11 She made this vow: "O Lord of hosts, if only you will look on the misery of your **servant**, and remember me, and not forget your **servant**, but will give to your servant a male child, then I will set him before you as a nazirite until the day of his death. He shall drink neither wine nor

---

[105] Matthew Leonard, *The Bible and the Virgin Mary Journey Through Scripture*, Participant Workbook (Steubenville: St. Paul Center for Biblical Theology, 2014), 28.

	intoxicants, and no razor shall touch his head."
Luke 1:46-55 NRSV	**1 Samuel 2:1-11**
And Mary said, "My soul magnifies the Lord, 47 and my spirit rejoices in God my Savior, 48 for he has looked with favor on the lowliness of his servant. Surely, from now on all generations will call me blessed; 49 for the Mighty One has done great things for me, and holy is his name. 50 His mercy is for those who fear him from generation to generation. 51 He has shown strength with his arm; he has scattered the proud in the thoughts of their hearts. 52 He has brought down the powerful from their thrones, and lifted up the lowly; 53 he has filled the hungry with good things, and sent the rich away empty. 54 He has helped his servant Israel, in remembrance of his mercy, 55 according to the promise he made to our ancestors, to Abraham and to his descendants forever."	1 Hannah prayed and said, "My heart exults in the Lord; my strength is exalted in my God. My mouth derides my enemies, because I rejoice in my victory. 2 There is no Holy One like the Lord, no one besides you; there is no Rock like our God. 3 Talk no more so very proudly, let not arrogance come from your mouth; for the Lord is a God of knowledge, and by him actions are weighed. 4 The bows of the mighty are broken, but the feeble gird on strength. 5 Those who were full have hired themselves out for bread, but those who were hungry are fat with spoil. The barren has borne seven, but she who has many children is forlorn. 6 The Lord kills and brings to life; he brings down to Sheol and raises up. 7 The Lord makes poor and makes rich; he brings low, he also exalts. 8 He raises

	up the poor from the dust; he lifts the needy from the ash heap, to make them sit with princes and inherit a seat of honor. For the pillars of the earth are the Lord's, and on them he has set the world. 9 He will guard the feet of his faithful ones, but the wicked shall be cut off in darkness; for not by might does one prevail. 10 The Lord! His adversaries shall be shattered; the Most High will thunder in heaven. The Lord will judge the ends of the earth; he will give strength to his king, and exalt the power of his anointed."

Wedding at Cana

At the wedding of Cana, Mary relates to her son Jesus in a similar way as Bathsheba, see below, relates to her son Solomon in his court. (Remember, according to a Jewish tradition, King Lemuel was considered Solomon.)[106] Both Mary and Bathsheba are the mothers of the men from whom

---

[106] Matthew Leonard, *The Bible and the Virgin Mary Journey Through Scripture*, 5 DVDs (Steubenville: St. Paul Center for Biblical Theology, 2014).

they ask help. Both Mary and Bathsheba intercede on behalf of others. Both are heard by their sons and their requests are granted.[107]

John 2:1-11	1 Kings 2:19-21 NRSV
On the third day there was a wedding in Cana of Galilee, and the mother of Jesus was there. 2 Jesus and his disciples had also been invited to the wedding. 3 When the wine gave out, **the mother of Jesus said to him, "They have no wine."** 4 And Jesus said to her, "Woman, what concern is that to you and to me? My hour has not yet come." 5 His mother said to the servants, **"Do whatever he tells you."** 6 Now standing there were six stone water jars for the Jewish rites of purification, each holding twenty or thirty gallons. 7 Jesus said to them, "Fill the jars with water." And they filled	So Bathsheba went to King Solomon, to speak to him on behalf of Adonijah. The king rose to meet her, and bowed down to her; then he sat on his throne, and had a throne brought for the king's mother, and she sat on his right. 20 Then she said, "**I have one small request to make of you; do not refuse me.**" And the king said to her, "**Make your request, my mother; for I will not refuse you.**" 21 She said, "Let Abishag the Shunammite be given to your brother Adonijah as his wife."
	Proverbs 31
	The words of King Lemuel. An oracle that his mother taught him: No, my son! No, son of my womb! No, son of my vows! Do not give your strength to women, your

---

[107] Matthew Leonard, *The Bible and the Virgin Mary Journey Through Scripture*, 5 DVDs (Steubenville: St. Paul Center for Biblical Theology, 2014).

them up to the brim. 8 He said to them, "Now draw some out, and take it to the chief steward." So they took it. 9 When the steward tasted the water that had become wine, and did not know where it came from (though the servants who had drawn the water knew), the steward called the bridegroom 10 and said to him, "Everyone serves the good wine first, and then the inferior wine after the guests have become drunk. But you have kept the good wine until now." 11 Jesus did this, the first of his signs, in Cana of Galilee, and revealed his glory; and his disciples believed in him.

ways to those who destroy kings. It is not for kings, O Lemuel, it is not for kings to drink wine, or for rulers to desire strong drink; or else they will drink and forget what has been decreed, and will pervert the rights of all the afflicted. **Give strong drink to one who is perishing, and wine to those in bitter distress**; let them drink and forget their poverty, and remember their misery no more. Speak out for those who cannot speak, for the rights of all the destitute. Speak out, judge righteously, defend the rights of the poor and needy.

Pentecost

At Pentecost a New Israel, the Catholic Church, was born. Mary helped to bring about this birth in a similar way as she gave birth to Jesus who was conceived by the Holy Spirit. In explaining the relationship of the Annunciation with Pentecost, in light of the birth of the Church, John Paul II writes:

> And so, in the redemptive economy of grace, brought about through the action of the Holy Spirit, there is a unique correspondence between the moment of the Incarnation of the Word and the moment of the birth of the Church. The person who links these two moments is Mary: Mary at Nazareth and Mary in the Upper Room at Jerusalem. In both cases her discreet yet essential presence indicates the path of "birth from the Holy Spirit." Thus she who is present in the mystery of Christ as Mother becomes-by the will of the Son and the power of the Holy Spirit-present in the mystery of the Church. In the Church too she continues to be a maternal presence, as is shown by the words spoken from the Cross: "Woman, behold your son!"; "Behold, your mother."[108]

The specific text from Scripture on Pentecost that John Paul is referring to is Acts chapter one

---

[108] John Paul II, "Redemptoris Mater," no. 24, w2.vatican.va, http://w2.vatican.va/content/john-paul-ii/en/encyclicals/documents/hf_jp-ii_enc_25031987_redemptoris-mater.html, (accessed June 2, 2016).

and chapter two. "Then they returned to Jerusalem .... When they had entered the city, they went to the room upstairs where they were staying, Peter, and John, and James, and Andrew, Philip and Thomas, Bartholomew and Matthew, James son of Alphaeus, and Simon the Zealot, and Judas son of James. All these were constantly devoting themselves to prayer, together with certain women, including Mary the mother of Jesus, as well as his brothers." (Acts 1:12-14 NRSV)

The descent of the Holy Apostles on the day of Pentecost in Acts chapter two is to be understood within the context of the Apostles gathered in prayer around Mary, the Mother of Jesus. Ratzinger, in describing the Marian context of Pentecost, writes, "That prayerful recollection we identified as characteristic of her nature once again becomes the space in which the Holy Spirit can enter and bring about a new creation."[109] At the Annunciation, Mary provided pristine "space" for the Holy Spirit to bring about Jesus in her womb. Her fiat, her unconditional yes to the Holy Spirit, was the condition for her to be the Mother of God. At Pentecost, Mary became the Mother of the Church by once again providing the Holy Spirit a space for the Holy Spirit to bring about the Church, as a new creation, a new people of God.

John Paul II calls this Marian "space" an

---

[109] Ratzinger, J., & von Balthasar, H. U. (2005). *Mary: The Church at the Source.* (A. Walker, Trans.) (pp. 73–74). San Francisco: Ignatius Press.

"interior space."[110] In commenting on this Marian terminology of John Paul II, which Ratzinger also uses, Antoine Nachef writes:

> From a Marian perspective, the faith of Mary becomes the first opportunity to provide a spiritual space between God and humankind that is not filled with evil. By "evil" is meant the evil in all its forms – diabolical, physical, and moral. This space, which is not a physical space, describes the manner of the relationship between God and humankind based on the distance and the difference between them as a transcendent God and a limited human person. ... When the Father looks at the faith of Mary in obeying the plan of the Incarnation, a new spiritual space is opened that can be filled with the blessing mentioned at the beginning of the Letter to the Ephesians.[111]

---

[110] John Paul II, "Redemptoris Mater," no. 28, w2.vatican.va, http://w2.vatican.va/content/john-paul-ii/en/encyclicals/documents/hf_jp-ii_enc_25031987_redemptoris-mater.html (accessed June 2, 2016).

[111] Antoine Nachef, *Mary's Pope: John Paul II, Mary, and the Church Since Vatican II* (Franklin: Sheed & Ward, 2000), 93.

Both Ratzinger's and John Paul II's connection of Mary at Pentecost with the Birth of the Church is a further development of what Vatican Council II taught in *Ad Gentes*, "[It] was from Pentecost that the 'Acts of the Apostles' took again, just as Christ was - conceived when the Holy Spirit came upon the Virgin Mary."[112]

At the Foot of the Cross

According to John Paul II, Mary's Motherhood of the Church began at the Annunciation by saying yes to God and by receiving the Holy Spirit into her immaculate "interior space." She then gave birth to the head of the Church who is Christ. At Pentecost, she once again acts as Mother to the Mystical Body of Christ, the Church, by providing her "interior space" to the Holy Spirit. Her spiritual motherhood of the Church present at Pentecost, though, was also "fully" present at the foot of the cross when, writes John Paul II, "an interior space was reopened within humanity which the eternal Father can fill 'with every spiritual blessing.' It is the space 'of the new and eternal Covenant,'-and it continues to exist in the Church, which in Christ is 'a kind of sacrament or sign of intimate union with God, and

---

[112] Vatican II, "Ad Gentes," no. 4, Vatican.va, http://www.vatican.va/archive/hist_councils/ii_vatican_coun cil/documents/vat-ii_decree_19651207_ad-gentes_en.html, (accessed May 15, 2016).

of the unity of all mankind.'"[113]

Nachef, in explaining John Paul II's thought, writes that the interior space of Mary which was "filled with every blessing opens a new possibility of union between God and humanity through Mary and extends that possibility to the Church."[114] Von Balthasar, as presented by Brendon Leahy, further clarifies Mary's maternal role as Mother of the Church by showing how at foot of the cross, and at Pentecost, Mary becomes not only God's spouse as Daughter Zion "the Bride turned toward the Bridegroom" but also, in participation of "Christ's universal outreach, Virgin-Mother open to everyone, including sinners."[115]

At the Annunciation, the accent is on Mary's yes as Bride turned unreservedly towards her Bridegroom, God. At the foot of the cross, the accent is on Mary as Virgin-Mother, who opens her arms wide to all, as represented by Bernini's colonnades in Rome. The first person she welcomed as Mother of the Church while at the foot of the cross was the Apostle John. Through the Apostle John, and in

---

[113] John Paul II, "Redemptoris Mater," no. 28, w2.vatican.va, http://w2.vatican.va/content/john-paul-ii/en/encyclicals/documents/hf_jp-ii_enc_25031987_redemptoris-mater.html, (accessed May 15, 2016).

[114] Antoine Nachef, *Mary's Pope: John Paul II, Mary, and the Church Since Vatican II* (Franklin: Sheed & Ward, 2000), 94.

[115] Brendan Leahy, *The Marian Profile* (New York: New City Press, 2000), 145. In reference to *Explorations III: Creator Spirit*, 113.

Christ, "Mary embraces each and every one in the Church".[116] John Paul II sheds light on this mystery by writing:

> At the foot of the Cross, when she accepts John as her son, when she asks, together with Christ, forgiveness from the Father for those who do not know what they do (cf. Lk 23:34), Mary experiences, in perfect docility to the Spirit, the richness and the universality of God's love, which opens her heart and enables it to embrace the entire human race. Thus Mary becomes Mother of each and every one of us, the Mother who obtains for us divine mercy.[117]

Woman of Revelation

Traditionally, the Woman of Revelation in

---

[116] John Paul II, "Redemptoris Mater," no. 47, w2.vatican.va, http://w2.vatican.va/content/john-paul-ii/en/encyclicals/documents/hf_jp-ii_enc_25031987_redemptoris-mater.html, (accessed May 15, 2016); cf. Antoine Nachef, *Mary's Pope: John Paul II, Mary, and the Church Since Vatican II* (Franklin: Sheed & Ward, 2000), 104.

[117] John Paul II, "Veritatis Splendor," no. 120, w2.vatican.va, http://w2.vatican.va/content/john-paul-ii/en/encyclicals/documents/hf_jp-ii_enc_06081993_veritatis-splendor.html, (accessed May 15, 2016).

chapter twelve of the Book of Revelation is identified with Mary. In addition, this woman in chapter twelve is understood as the fulfillment of the woman described in Genesis chapter three. A comparison between these two passages is below. In Revelation chapter twelve, the serpent of Genesis chapter three, verse fifteen is interpreted as Satan, the woman as Mary, and her offspring, as Jesus. Since, according to Catholic doctrine, points out Matthew Leonard, Mary was conceived immaculately she, consequently, did not fall under the power of Satan. This, then, allows her, by her son, to defeat Satan since he cannot control her.[118] In identifying Mary both with the woman in the third chapter of Genesis and the woman in the twelfth chapter of Revelation, John Paul II writes:

> Thanks to this special bond linking the Mother of Christ with the Church, there is further clarified the mystery of that "woman" who, from the first chapters of the Book of Genesis until the Book of Revelation, accompanies the revelation of God's salvific plan for humanity. For Mary, present in the Church as the Mother of the Redeemer, takes part, as a

---

[118] Matthew Leonard, *The Bible and the Virgin Mary Journey Through Scripture*, Participant Workbook (Steubenville: St. Paul Center for Biblical Theology, 2014), 98; Scott Hahn, *Hail, Holy Queen* (New York: Image Books, 2001), 60;

mother, in that monumental struggle; against the powers of darkness" which continues throughout human history. And by her ecclesial identification as the "woman clothed with the sun" (Rev. 12:1), it can be said that "in the Most Holy Virgin the Church has already reached that perfection whereby she exists without spot or wrinkle."[119]

Genesis 3:15 NRSV	Revelation 12:1-6 NRSV
I will put enmity between you and the **woman**, and between your **offspring** and hers; he will strike your head, and you will strike his heel.	1 A great portent appeared in heaven: a **woman** clothed with the sun, with the moon under her feet, and on her head a crown of twelve stars. 2 She was pregnant and was crying out in birth pangs, in the agony of giving birth. 3 Then another portent appeared in heaven: a great red dragon, with seven heads and ten

[119] John Paul II, "Redemptoris Mater," no. 47, w2.vatican.va, http://w2.vatican.va/content/john-paul-ii/en/encyclicals/documents/hf_jp-ii_enc_25031987_redemptoris-mater.html, (accessed May 15, 2016); John Paul II, "Mary is Church's Pattern, Angelus, 15 August 1995," ewtn.com, https://www.ewtn.com/library/PAPALDOC/JP950815.HTM (accessed June 2, 2016).

	horns, and seven diadems on his heads. 4 His tail swept down a third of the stars of heaven and threw them to the earth. Then the dragon stood before the woman who was about to bear a child, so that he might devour her child as soon as it was born. 5 And she **gave birth to a son**, a male child, who is to rule all the nations with a rod of iron. But her child was snatched away and taken to God and to his throne; 6 and the woman fled into the wilderness, where she has a place prepared by God, so that there she can be nourished for one thousand two hundred sixty days.

A close examination of the Revelation chapter twelve and the preceding chapter also reveals other aspects from the Old Testament that are fulfilled in Mary. In order to see how Revelation chapter eleven is fulfilled in Mary, it is necessary to point out that originally the book of Revelation did not have chapter divisions. Consequently, the last verses of chapter eleven and the first verses of chapter twelve do not necessarily mean that John intended them to be interpreted as two distinct units. Instead, as we will see, they are related to one another.

Revelation eleven, verse nineteen, describes heaven opening and the ark of the covenant appearing, which Jeremiah (2 Maccabees 2:7-8) prophesied would happen. In chapter twelve, we are told that the ark is a woman, who in Catholic tradition is Mary. Mary is accompanied by images that Jeremiah prophesied would be present when the ark is once again revealed: the glory of the Lord and a celestial signs related to a cloud.[120] These and other New Testament fulfillments are pointed out by Matthew Leonard. Some of his scriptural comparisons are below.

Old Testament Type	New Testament Fulfillment
2 Maccabees 2:7-8 "When Jeremiah learned of it, he rebuked them and declared: "The place shall remain unknown until God gathers his people together again and shows his mercy. Then the Lord will disclose these things, and the glory of the Lord and the cloud will appear,	Revelation 11:19 "Then God's temple in heaven was opened, and the ark of his covenant was seen within his temple; and there were flashes of lightning, rumblings, peals of thunder, an earthquake, and heavy hail."

---

[120] Matthew Leonard, *The Bible and the Virgin Mary Journey Through Scripture*, Participant Workbook (Steubenville: St. Paul Center for Biblical Theology, 2014), 117-118.

as they were shown in the case of Moses, and as Solomon asked that the place should be specially consecrated."	
Queen Bride of Israel (Is. 60:19-20; 62:3-5, Song 6:10)	Queen Bride of the New Israel and the New Queen Mother who sits by her son Jesus. Revelation 12:1 "woman clothed with the sun"
The Twelve Tribes of Israel	Mary is surrounded by the New Israel represented by twelve stars corresponding to the Twelve Apostles. Revelation 12:1 "on her head a crown of twelve stars".

121

One final note, since, according to Catholic tradition, Mary did not suffer from physical birth pangs due to her being immaculately conceived and was exempt from the penalties associated with original sin (Genesis 3:16), how can Mary be identified with the Woman of Revelation? After all, the Woman of Revelation is described as suffering from birth pangs. This is answered by distinguishing physical birth pangs from spiritual birth pangs. The birth pangs described in Revelation

---

121 Matthew Leonard, *The Bible and the Virgin Mary Journey Through Scripture*, Participant Workbook (Steubenville: St. Paul Center for Biblical Theology, 2014), 117-118.

chapter twelve are not describing Mary's physical birth pangs but rather the spiritual suffering she experienced when giving birth to Jesus. Von Balthasar identifies this spiritual suffering as the detachment from her intimacy with the Second Person of the Blessed Trinity which giving birth required from her. These detachment pains, further explains von Balthasar, anticipated the suffering she would experience at the foot of the cross.[122] In addition, Scott Hahn adds that St. Paul refers to birth pangs in a spiritual sense (Gal 4:19; Rom 8:22) as does Jesus (John 16:20-22).[123]

Discussion Questions

1. Typologically compare Mary at the Annunciation with Zephaniah 3:14, Exodus 40:34-35, and Genesis 18:13-14. Do so by comparing the Old Testament passages separately with the Annunciation scene.

2. Typologically compare Mary's visitation to her cousin Elizabeth with 2 Samuel 6:2-11, 1 Samuel 1:9-11, 1 Samuel 2:1-11. Do so by comparing the Old Testament passages separately with the Visitation scene.

---

[122] Brendan Leahy, *The Marian Profile* (New York: New City Press, 2000), 86.

[123] Scott Hahn, *Hail, Holy Queen* (New York: Image Books, 2001), 61-62.

3. Typologically compare Mary's presence at the Wedding at Cana with 1 Kings 2:19-21, and Proverbs 31. Do so by comparing the Old Testament passages separately with the Wedding at Cana.

4. Compare the Annunciation scene with Mary's presence at Pentecost, and with Mary at the foot of the cross. Include the following in your response: Holy Spirit, birth, interior space, Bride, and Mother.

5. Typologically compare the following passages: Genesis 3:15 with Revelation 12:1-6 and 2 Maccabees 2:7-8 with Revelation 11:19. Finally, explain how the Woman of Revelation represents Mary even though the Woman of Revelation experienced birth pangs.

Chapter 6

Patristics: Early Development

Introduction:

According to von Balthasar, Mary's presence during the early patristic era was hidden and even "anonymous."[124] After the Council of Nicaea (325 AD), Mary's role in theology began to emerge. Following von Balthasar's division, this chapter will first focus on Mary's role in theology before the Council of Nicaea, and then focus on her role after the Council of Nicaea.

Marian Theology Before the Council of Nicaea

The reason that von Balthasar gives for describing Mary's presence in the pre-Council of Nicaea as anonymous was that although the Church was identified as feminine, as a bride of Christ, and as a mother, the Church's relationship with Mary remained relatively undefined. For this reason, Mary is presented in the early patristic age as subordinate to the Church and only a favored

---

[124] Brendan Leahy, *The Marian Profile* (New York: New City Press, 2000), 21.

member of the Church.[125] To see this early patristic understanding of Mary, we will look briefly at Marian references in the following Church Fathers: Ignatius of Antioch, Justin Martyr, Irenaeus of Lyons, and Clement of Alexandria. This section will conclude with the ecclesiastical writer Origen who has recently been rehabilitated by the Church.[126]

127

---

[125] Brendan Leahy, *The Marian Profile* (New York: New City Press, 2000), 20-21.

[126] The same cannot be said of the influential ecclesiastical writer Tertullian (c. 155-240) since he broke from the Church to join the heretical group of Montanism.

[127] Not identified, *"Theotokos of Vladimir,"* photograph, https://commons.wikimedia.org/wiki/File:Vladi mirskaya.jpg (accessed June 27, 2016).

Ignatius of Antioch

Repeatedly throughout his writings, St. Ignatius of Antioch (c. 35-c. 108) refers to Mary as the Virgin. He also makes a distinction between Jesus being eternally begotten by the Father from Jesus' birth in time by the Virgin Mary. His birth by the Virgin Mary, asserts Ignatius, was an actual human birth, that fulfilled the prophecy of Isaiah, "the Lord himself will give you a sign. Look, the young woman is with child and shall bear a son, and shall name him Immanuel." (Isaiah 7: 14 NRSV)

> Glorify the God and Father of our Lord Jesus Christ, who by Him has given you such wisdom. For I have observed that ye are perfected in an immoveable faith, as if ye were nailed to the cross of our Lord Jesus Christ, both in the flesh and in the spirit, and are established in love through the blood of Christ, being fully persuaded, in very truth, with respect to our Lord Jesus Christ, that He was the Son of God, "the first-born of every creature," God the Word, the only-begotten Son, and was of the seed of David according to the flesh, **by the Virgin Mary**; was baptized by John, that all righteousness might be fulfilled by Him; that

He lived a life of holiness without sin, and was truly, under Pontius Pilate and Herod the tetrarch, nailed [to the cross] for us in His flesh. From whom we also derive our being, from His divinely-blessed passion, that He might set up a standard for the ages, through His resurrection, to all His holy and faithful [followers], whether among Jews or Gentiles, in the one body of His Church.[128]

Stop your ears, therefore, when any one speaks to you at variance with Jesus Christ, the Son of God, who was descended from David, and was also of Mary; who was truly **begotten of God and of the Virgin, but not after the same manner**. For indeed God and man are not the same. He truly assumed a body; for "the Word was made flesh," and lived upon earth without sin.[129]

---

[128] Ignatius of Antioch, "The Epistle of Ignatius to the Smyrnaeans," chap. 1 earlychristianwritings.com, http://www.earlychristianwritings.com/text/ignatius-smyrnaeans-longer.html, (accessed June 4, 2016).

[129] Ignatius of Antioch, "Epistle of Ignatius to the Trallians," chap. 9, earlychristianwritings.com, http://www.earlychristianwritings.com/text/ignatius-trallians-longer.html, (accessed June 4, 2016).

These things [I address to you], my beloved, not that I know any of you to be in such a state; but, as less than any of you, I desire to guard you beforehand, that ye fall not upon the hooks of vain doctrine, but that you may rather attain to a full assurance in Christ, who was **begotten by the Father** before all ages, but was **afterwards born of the Virgin Mary** without any intercourse with man.[130]

But as for me, I do not place my hopes in one who died for me in appearance, but in reality. For that which is false is quite abhorrent to the truth. Mary then did truly conceive a body which had God inhabiting it. And God the Word was truly born of the Virgin, having clothed Himself with a body of like passions with our own. He who forms all men in the womb, was Himself really in the womb, and made for Himself a body of the seed of the Virgin, but **without any**

---

[130] Ignatius of Antioch, "Ignatius to the Magnesians," chap. 11, earlychristianwritings.com, http://www.earlychristianwritings.com/text/ignatius-magnesians-longer.html, (accessed June 4, 2016).

intercourse of man. He was carried in the womb, even as we are, for the usual period of time; and **was really born**, as we also are; and was in reality nourished with milk, and partook of common meat and drink, even as we do.[131]

The cross of Christ is indeed a stumbling-block to those that do not believe, but to the believing it is salvation and life eternal. "Where is the wise man? where the disputer? " Where is the boasting of those who are called mighty? For the Son of God, who was begotten before time began, and established all things according to the will of the Father, He was conceived in the womb of Mary, according to the appointment of God, of the seed of David, and by the Holy Ghost. **For says [the Scripture], "Behold, a virgin shall be with child,** and shall bring forth a son, and He shall be called Immanuel." He was born and was baptized by John, that He might ratify the institution committed to

---

[131] Ignatius of Antioch, "Epistle of Ignatius to the Trallians," chap. 10, earlychristianwritings.com, http://www.earlychristianwritings.com/text/ignatius-trallians-longer.html, (accessed June 4, 2016).

that prophet.[132]

Justin Martyr

Along with teaching that Jesus was truly born of a virgin, St. Justin Martyr (c. 100-c.165) emphasizes in his writings the obedience of the Virgin Mary in contrast to the disobedience of the virgin Eve. Justin Martyr and others refer interchangeably to the Virgin Mother the Church and the Virgin Mother Mary. Mary's motherhood of the Church, though, at this early stage was mainly implied.[133]

> And our Lord **Jesus Christ was born of a virgin**, for no other reason than that He might destroy the begetting by lawless desire, and might show to the ruler that the formation of man was possible to God without human intervention. And when He had been born, and had submitted to the other conditions of the flesh,--I mean food, drink, and clothing,--this one condition only of discharging the sexual function He did not submit to; for,

[132] Ignatius of Antioch, "Ignatius to the Ephesians," chaps. 18, earlychristianwritings.com, http://www.earlychristianwritings.com/text/ignatius-ephesians-longer.html, (accessed June 4, 2016).

[133] Brendan Leahy, *The Marian Profile* (New York: New City Press, 2000), 20.

regarding the desires of the flesh, He accepted some as necessary, while others, which were unnecessary, He did not submit to. For if the flesh were deprived of food, drink, and clothing, it would be destroyed; but being deprived of lawless desire, it suffers no harm. And at the same time He foretold that, in the future world, sexual intercourse should be done away with; as He says, "The children of this world marry, and are given in marriage; but the children of the world to come neither marry nor are given in marriage, but shall be like the angels in heaven." Let not, then, those that are unbelieving marvel, if in the world to come He do away with those acts of our fleshly members which even in this present life are abolished.[134]

Now it is evident to all, that in the race of Abraham according to the flesh no one has been born of a virgin, or is said to have been born [of a virgin], save this our Christ. But since you and your teachers venture

---

[134] Justin Martyr, "Fragments of the Lost Work of Justin on the Resurrection," chap. 3, earlychristianwritings.com, http://www.earlychristianwritings.com/text/justinmartyr-resurrection.html, (accessed June 4, 2016).

to affirm that in the prophecy of Isaiah it is not said, 'Behold, the virgin shall conceive,' but, **'Behold, the young woman shall conceive, and bear a son**;' and [since] you explain the prophecy as if [it referred] to Hezekiah, who was your king, I shall endeavor to [discuss shortly this point in opposition to you, and to show that reference is made to Him who is **acknowledged by us as Christ**."[135]

He became man by the Virgin, in order that the disobedience which proceeded from the serpent might receive its destruction in the same manner in which it derived its origin. For **Eve**, **who was a virgin** and undefiled, having conceived the word of the serpent, brought forth disobedience and death. But the

---

[135] Justin Martyr, "Dialogue with Trypho," earlychristianwritings.com, http://www.earlychristianwritings.com/text/justinmartyr-dialoguetrypho.html, (accessed June 4, 2016); cf. Justin Martyr, "The First Apology of Justin," chap. 33, earlychristianwritings.com, http://www.earlychristianwritings.com/text/justinmartyr-firstapology.html, (accessed June 4, 2016).

> **Virgin Mary** received faith and joy, when the angel Gabriel announced the good tidings to her that the Spirit of the Lord would come upon her, and the power of the Highest would overshadow her: wherefore also the Holy Thing begotten of her is the Son of God; and she replied, 'Be it unto me according to thy word.'[136]

Irenaeus of Lyons (c.120-c.202)

Like St. Justin Martyr, St. Irenaeus (c. 120-202) also draws attention to the obedience of the Virgin Mary in contrast with the disobedience of the virgin Eve. He does so, though, by further developing this typology and in so doing making it clearer. Irenaeus's words on Mary also differ from St. Justin Martyr's when "in," describes von Balthasar, "a flash of intuition"[137] he nearly identifies Mary with the Church.[138]

> In accordance with this design, Mary the Virgin is found obedient, saying, "Behold the handmaid of the Lord;

---

[136] Justin Martyr, "Dialogue with Trypho," chap. C, earlychristianwritings.com, http://www.earlychristianwritings.com/text/justinmartyr-dialoguetrypho.html, (accessed June 4, 2016).

[137] Brendan Leahy, *The Marian Profile* (New York: New City Press, 2000), 22.

[138] Brendan Leahy, *The Marian Profile* (New York: New City Press, 2000), 22.

be it unto me according to thy word." But Eve was disobedient; for she did not obey when as yet she was a virgin. And even as she, having indeed a husband, Adam, but being nevertheless as yet a virgin (for in Paradise "they were both naked, and were not ashamed," inasmuch as they, having been created a short time previously, had no understanding of the procreation of children: for it was necessary that they should first come to adult age, and then multiply from that time onward), having become disobedient, was made the cause of death, both to herself and to the entire human race; so also did Mary, having a man betrothed [to her], and being nevertheless a virgin, by yielding obedience, become the cause of salvation, both to herself and the whole human race. ... And thus also it was that the **knot of Eve's disobedience was loosed by the obedience of Mary**. For what the virgin Eve had bound fast through unbelief, this did the virgin Mary set free through faith.[139]

---

[139] Irenaeus, "Against Heresies," bk. III, chap. 22, no. 4, earlychristianwritings.com,

"But at that time the angel Gabriel
was sent from God, who did also say
to the virgin, Fear not, Mary; for
thou hast found favour with God." ...
And **Mary**, exulting because of this,
cried out, **prophesying on behalf
of the Church**, "My soul doth
magnify the Lord, and my spirit hath
rejoiced in God my Saviour. For He
hath taken up His child Israel, in
remembrance of His mercy, as He
spake to our fathers, Abraham, and
his seed forever."[140]

Clement of Alexandria

St. Clement of Alexandria (c. 150-c.215) interchangeably refers to Mary as the virgin mother and
the Church as a virgin mother that seem to indicate
they are in a certain sense identified:

[P]regnant women, on becoming
mothers, discharge milk. **But the**

http://www.earlychristianwritings.com/irenaeus.html,
(accessed June 5, 2016); cf. "Lumen Gentium," no. 56,
Vatican.va, http://www.vatican.va/archive/hist_councils/
ii_vatican_council/documents/vat-ii_const_19641121_lumen-
gentium_en.html, (accessed May 30, 2016).

[140] Irenaeus of Lyons, "Against Heresies," bk. 3, chap. 10,
no. 2, earlychristianwritings.com,
http://www.earlychristianwritings.com/text/irenaeus-
book3.html, (accessed June 5, 2016).

Lord Christ, the fruit of the Virgin, did not pronounce the breasts of women blessed, nor selected them to give nourishment; but when the kind and loving Father had rained down the Word, Himself became spiritual nourishment to the good. O mystic marvel! The universal Father is one, and one the universal Word; and the Holy Spirit is one and the same everywhere, and **one is the only virgin mother. I love to call her the Church**. This mother, when alone, had not milk, because alone she was not a woman. But she is once virgin and mother--pure as a virgin, loving as a mother. And calling her children to her, she nurses them with holy milk, viz., with the Word for childhood. Therefore, she had not milk; for the milk was this child fair and comely, the body of Christ, which nourishes by the Word the young brood, which the Lord Himself brought forth in throes of the flesh, which the Lord Himself swathed in His precious blood.[141]

---

[141] Clement of Alexandria, "The Instructor," bk. 1, chap. 6, earlychristianwritings.com,

Origen

The ecclesiastical writer Origen (c. 185-c.254) also relates Mary to the Church by identifying her as our universal mother. Another theme from Origin that will be further developed with reference to Mary is the idea that the Church has a soul.[142]

> But Luke, though he says at the beginning of Acts, "The former treatise did I make about all that Jesus began to do and to teach," yet leaves to him who lay on Jesus' breast the greatest and completest discourses about Jesus. For none of these plainly declared His Godhead, as John does when he makes Him say, "I am the light of the world," "I am the way and the truth and the life," "I am the resurrection, "I am the door," "I am the good shepherd;" and in the Apocalypse, "I am the Alpha and the Omega, the beginning and the end, the first and the last." We may therefore make bold to say that the Gospels are the first fruits of all the Scriptures, but that of the

---

http://www.earlychristianwritings.com/text/clement-instructor-book1.html, (accessed June 4, 2016).

[142] Brendan Leahy, *The Marian Profile* (New York: New City Press, 2000), 21-22.

Gospels that of John is the first fruits. **No one can apprehend the meaning of it except he have lain on Jesus' breast and received from Jesus Mary to be his mother also.** Such a one must he become who is to be another John, and to have shown to him, like John, by Jesus Himself Jesus as He is. For if Mary, as those declare who with sound mind extol her, had no other son but Jesus, and yet Jesus says to His mother, "Woman, behold thy son," and not "Behold you have this son also," then He virtually said to her, "Lo, this is Jesus, whom thou didst bear." Is it not the case that everyone who is perfect lives himself no longer, but Christ lives in him; and if Christ lives in him, then it is said of him to Mary, "Behold thy son Christ."[143]

[W]e say that the holy Scriptures declare the body of Christ, animated by the Son of God, to be the whole Church of God, and the members of

---

[143] Origen, "Origen. Commentary on John," bk. 1, 6, earlychristianwritings.com, http://www.earlychristianwritings.com/text/origen-john1.html, (accessed June 5, 2016).

this body--considered as a whole--to consist of those who are believers; since, **as a soul vivifies and moves the body**, which of itself has not the natural power of motion like a living being, **so the Word, arousing and moving the whole body, the Church**, to befitting action, awakens, moreover, each individual member belonging to the Church, so that they do nothing apart from the Word. Since all this, then, follows by a train of reasoning not to be depreciated, where is the difficulty in maintaining that, as the soul of Jesus is joined in a perfect and inconceivable manner with the very Word, so the person of Jesus, generally speaking, is not separated from the only-begotten and first-born of all creation, and is not a different being from Him? But enough here on this subject.[144]

Marian Theology After the Council of Nicaea

Two early councils that significantly helped to advance Marian theology were the Council of

---

[144] Origen, "Origen. Contra Celsus," bk. VI, chap. 48, earlychristianwritings.com, http://www.earlychristianwritings.com/text/origen166.html, (accessed June 5, 2016).

Nicaea (325), which taught Christ is one with (consubstantial) the Father, and the Council of Ephesus (431), which taught that Mary is the Mother of God (*Theotokos*). "If anyone will not confess that the Emmanuel is very God, and that therefore the Holy Virgin is the Mother of God (Θεοτόκος), inasmuch as in the flesh she bore the Word of God made flesh [as it is written, "The Word was made flesh"] let him be anathema."[145]

Along with teaching that Mary is the Mother of God, Church Fathers after this council also taught Mary is the New Ark, fulfills the role of Moses's sister Miriam, personifies the Church, and is the location for a New Creation. Despite, however, the significant development of Marian theology during the later portion of the Patristic age, Mary's relationship to the Church still needed to be clarified. This is evident, von Balthasar points out, in Augustine's Marian minimalism in which Mary is depicted on a parallel track to the Church, but is not identified with the Church.[146]

Athanasius (c. 296-c. 373)

St. Athanasius (c. 296-c. 373) vigorously defended Mary as a virgin Mother of God:

---

[145] "Council of Ephesus," xii, anathematisms of St. Cyril Against Nestorius, ccel.org, http://www.ccel.org/ccel/schaff/npnf214.x.ix.i.html, (accessed May 5, 2016).

[146] Brendan Leahy, *The Marian Profile* (New York: New City Press, 2000), 23-24.

Nor did He will merely to become embodied or merely to appear; had that been so, He could have revealed His divine majesty in some other and better way. No, He took our body, and not only so, but **He took it directly from a spotless, stainless virgin**, without the agency of human father—a pure body, untainted by intercourse with man. He, the Mighty One, the Artificer of all, Himself prepared this body in the virgin as a temple for Himself, and took it for His very own, as the instrument through which He was known and in which He dwelt.[147]

Many for instance have been made holy and clean from all sin; nay, Jeremiah was hallowed even from the womb, and John, while yet in the womb, leapt for joy at the voice of **Mary Bearer of God [θεο- τόκου];** nevertheless 'death reigned from Adam to Moses, even over those that had not sinned after the similitude of Adam's transgress-

---

[147] Athanasius, "On the Incarnation," chap. 2, no. 8, ccel.org, http://www.ccel.org/ccel/athanasius/incarnation.pdf, (accessed June 5, 2016).

sion;' and thus man remained mortal and corruptible as before, liable to the affections proper to their nature. But now the Word having become man and having appropriated what pertains to the flesh, no longer do these things touch the body, because of the Word who has come in it, but they are destroyed by Him, and henceforth men no longer remain sinners and dead according to their proper affections, but having risen according to the Word's power, they abide ever immortal and incorruptible. Whence also, whereas the flesh is born of Mary Bearer of God, He Himself is said to have been born, who furnishes to others an origin of being; in order that He may transfer our origin into Himself, and we may no longer, as mere earth, return to earth, but as being knit into the Word from heaven, may be carried to heaven by Him.[148]

Ephrem the Syrian (c. 306-373)

Due to his composition of beautiful and truth-

---

[148] Athanasius, "Against the Arians," discourse III, chap. 26, no. 33, p. 1039, ccel.org, http://www.ccel.org/ccel/schaff/npnf204.html, (accessed June 5, 2016).

filled spiritual poetry and hymns, St. Ephrem the Syrian (c. 306-373) is commonly known as the Harp of the Holy Spirit.[149] Below, he describes Mary as an ark, carrying Jesus, ministered by Joseph:

> The woman ministers before the man, because he is her head. Joseph rose to minister before his Lord, Who was in Mary. The priest ministered before Your ark by reason of Your holiness.[150]

Gregory of Nazianzus (329-389)

St. Gregory of Nazianzus (329-389) was one of the three Cappadocian Fathers, the others being St. Basil the Great and St. Gregory of Nyssa.

> If anyone does not believe that Holy **Mary is the Mother of God**, he is severed from the Godhead. If anyone should assert that He passed through the Virgin as through a channel, and was not at once divinely and humanly formed in her

---

[149] Benedict XVI, "Saint Ephrem," General Audience, Wednesday, November 28, 2007, w2.vatican.va, http://w2.vatican.va/content/benedict-xvi/en/audiences/2007/documents/hf_ben-xvi_aud_20071128.html, (accessed June 5, 2016).

[150] Ephraim the Syrian, "Hymns on the Nativity," Hymn 11, newadvent.org, http://www.newadvent.org/fathers/3703.htm, (accessed June 5, 2016).

(divinely, because without the intervention of a man; humanly, because in accordance with the laws of gestation), he is in like manner godless. If any assert that the Manhood was formed and afterward was clothed with the Godhead, he too is to be condemned. For this were not a Generation of God, but a shirking of generation. If any introduce the notion of Two Sons, one of God the Father, the other of the Mother, and discredits the Unity and Identity, may he lose his part in the adoption promised to those who believe aright. For God and Man are two natures, as also soul and body are; but there are not two Sons or two Gods. For neither in this life are there two manhoods; though Paul speaks in some such language of the inner and outer man. And (if I am to speak concisely) the Savior is made of elements which are distinct from one another (for the invisible is not the same with the visible, nor the timeless with that which is subject to time), yet He is not two Persons. God forbid! For both natures are one by the combination, the Deity being made Man, and the Manhood deified or however one should express it. And I say different Elements, because it is the reverse of what is the case in the Trinity; for There we acknowledge different Persons so as not to confound the persons; but not different Elements, for the Three are One and the same in Godhead.[151]

Basil the Great (c. 330-379)

St. Basil the Great, alternatively known as Basil of Caesarea, likewise defended Mary as Mother of God.[152] In one of his writings, he connects her Motherhood of God with the oral tradition of her perpetual virginity.

> For "he did not know her"-it says- "until she gave birth to a Son, her firstborn" (Mt 1:25). But this could make one suppose that Mary, after having offered in all purity her own service in giving birth to the Lord, by virtue of the intervention of the Holy Spirit, did not subsequently refrain

---

[151] Gregory Nazianzen, "Letters (Division I): To Cledonius the Priest Against Apollinarius (Ep. CI.)," newadvent.org, http://www.newadvent.org/fathers/3103a.htm, (accessed June 5, 2016).

[152] Luigi Gambero, *Mary and the Fathers of the Church: The Blessed Virgin Mary in Patristic Thought*, trans. Thomas Buffer (San Francisco: Ignatius Press, 1991), 145. The following is cited. *On the Holy Generation of Christ* 3; PG 31, 1464 A.

from normal conjugal relations.

That would not have affected the teaching of our religion at all, because Mary's virginity was necessary until the service of the Incarnation, and what happened afterward need not be investigated in order to affect the doctrine of the mystery.

But since the lovers of Christ [that is, the faithful] do not allow themselves to hear that the Mother of God (*Theotokos*) ceased at a given moment to be a virgin, we consider their testimony to be sufficient.[153]

Gregory of Nyssa

The third Cappadocian Father St. Gregory of Nyssa (c. 330-c. 395), the younger brother of Basil the Great, defends the tradition of Mary's Perpetual Virginity with the possible explanation that she took a vow of virginity. According to Luigi Gambero, Gregory of Nyssa may be the first to refer

---

[153] Luigi Gambero, *Mary and the Fathers of the Church: The Blessed Virgin Mary in Patristic Thought*, trans. Thomas Buffer (San Francisco: Ignatius Press, 1991), 146. The following is cited. *On the Holy Generation of Christ* 3; PG 31, 1468 B.

in writing to this tradition.[154] Another connection that Gregory of Nyssa made is the typological association between Moses's sister Miriam and Mary.

> What is Mary's response? Listen to the voice of the pure Virgin. The angel brings the glad tidings of childbearing, but she is concerned with virginity and holds that her integrity should come before the angelic message. She does not refuse to believe the angel; neither does she move away from her convictions. She says: I have given up any contact with man. "How will this happen to me, since I do not know man?" (Lk 1:34).

> **Mary's own words confirm certain apocryphal traditions**. For if Joseph had taken her to be his wife, for the purpose of having children, why would she have wondered at the announcement of maternity, since she herself would have accepted becoming a mother according to the law of nature?

---

[154] Luigi Gambero, *Mary and the Fathers of the Church: The Blessed Virgin Mary in Patristic Thought*, trans. Thomas Buffer (San Francisco: Ignatius Press, 1991), 146.

But just as it was necessary to guard the body consecrated to God as an untouched and holy offering, for this same reason, she states, even if you are an angel come down from heaven and even if this phenomenon is beyond man's abilities, yet it is impossible for me to know man. How shall I become a mother without [knowing] man? For though I consider Joseph to be my husband, still I do not know man.[155]

But besides other things the action of **Miriam** the prophetess also gives rise to these surmisings of ours. Directly the sea was crossed she took in her hand a dry and sounding timbrel and conducted the women's dance. By this timbrel the story may mean to imply virginity, as first perfected by Miriam; whom indeed I would believe to be a **type of Mary the mother of God**. Just as the timbrel emits a loud sound because it is devoid of all moisture and reduced to the highest degree of

---

[155] Luigi Gambero, *Mary and the Fathers of the Church: The Blessed Virgin Mary in Patristic Thought*, trans. Thomas Buffer (San Francisco: Ignatius Press, 1991), 157. The following is cited. *On the Holy Generation of Christ*, PG 46, 1140 C-1141 A.

dryness, so has virginity a clear and ringing report amongst men because it repels from itself the vital sap of merely physical life. Thus, Miriam's timbrel being a dead thing, and virginity being a deadening of the bodily passions, it is perhaps not very far removed from the bounds of probability that Miriam was a virgin. However, we can but guess and surmise, we cannot clearly prove, that this was so, and that Miriam the prophetess led a dance of virgins, even though many of the learned have affirmed distinctly that she was unmarried, from the fact that the history makes no mention either of her marriage or of her being a mother; and surely she would have been named and known, not as "the sister of Aaron," but from her husband, if she had had one; since the head of the woman is not the brother but the husband. But if, amongst a people with whom motherhood was sought after and classed as a blessing and regarded as a public duty, the grace of virginity, nevertheless, came to be regarded as a precious thing, how does it behove us to feel towards it, who do not "judge" of the Divine blessings "according to the flesh"?[156]

Ambrose of Milan (c. 340-397)

According to the early Christian scholar Luigi Gambero, St. Ambrose (c. 340-397) "is the first Christian author to call Mary the type and image of the Church."[157]

> Well [does the Gospel say]: married but a virgin; because **she is the type of the Church**, which is also married but remains immaculate. The Virgin [Church] conceived us by the Holy Spirit and, as a virgin, gave birth to us without pain. And perhaps this is why holy Mary, married to one man [Joseph], is made fruitful by another [the Holy Spirit], to show that the individual churches are filled with the Spirit and with grace, even as they are united to the person of a temporal priest.[158]

---

[156] Gregory of Nyssa, "NPNF2-05. Gregory of Nyssa: Dogmatic Treatises, etc." Ascetic and Moral, chap xix, ccel.org, http://www.ccel.org/ccel/schaff/npnf205html, (accessed June 5, 2016).

[157] Luigi Gambero, *Mary and the Fathers of the Church: The Blessed Virgin Mary in Patristic Thought*, trans. Thomas Buffer (San Francisco: Ignatius Press, 1991), 198.

[158] Luigi Gambero, *Mary and the Fathers of the Church: The Blessed Virgin Mary in Patristic Thought*, trans. Thomas Buffer (San Francisco: Ignatius Press, 1991), 198. Gambero cites the following. *Expositio in Lucam* 2, 7; PL 15, 1635-36

Jerome

St. Jerome (347-430) helps to establish the foundation for understanding Mary as providing the beginning of a new creation since her womb encompassed Christ, the New Adam. In commenting on the passage below by St. Jerome, Tim Staples writes, "If we examine the Old Testament, we discover it was the first man-*Adam*-who 'compassed' the woman-*Eve*, for she was created from him. In the recapitulation of all things in the New Covenant, God deigned to reverse this order just as he was to reverse the curse of original sin: Jesus, the 'second man' or 'second Adam,' comes from the new woman, Mary."[159]

> Let us hasten to the rest: Isaiah 37:22 The **virgin daughter of Zion** has despised you and laughed you to scorn. To her whom he called daughter the prophet also gave the title virgin, for fear that if he spoke only of a daughter, it might be supposed that she was married. This is the virgin daughter whom elsewhere he thus addresses: Isaiah 54:1 Sing, O barren, you that dost not bear; break forth into singing, and cry aloud, you that did not

[159] Tim Staples, *Behold Your Mother: A Biblical and Historical Defense of the Marian Doctrines* (El Cajon: Catholic Answers, Kindle Edition, 2014,) loc. 1217 of 6088.

travail with child: for more are the children of the desolate, than the children of the married wife, says the Lord. This is she of whom God by the mouth of Jeremiah speaks, saying: Jeremiah 2:32 Can a maid forget her ornaments, or a bride her attire. Concerning her we read of a great miracle in the same prophecy Jeremiah 31:22 — that a **woman should compass a man**, and that the **Father of all things should be contained in a virgin's womb**.[160]

---

[160] Jerome, "Against Jovinianus," bk, 1, no. 32, newadvent.org, http://www.newadvent.org/fathers/30091.htm, (accessed June 5, 2016). The text right before this passages provides important context. "Isaiah tells of the mystery of our faith and hope: Isaiah 7:14 Behold a virgin shall conceive, and bear a son, and shall call his name Emmanuel. I know that the Jews are accustomed to meet us with the objection that in Hebrew the word Almah does not mean a virgin, but a young woman. And, to speak truth, a virgin is properly called Bethulah, but a young woman, or a girl, is not Almah, but Naarah! What then is the meaning of Almah? A hidden virgin, that is, not merely virgin, but a virgin and something more, because not every virgin is hidden, shut off from the occasional sight of men. Then again, Rebecca, on account of her extreme purity, and because she was a type of the Church which she represented in her own virginity, is described in Genesis as Almah, not Bethulah, as may clearly be proved from the words of Abraham's servant, spoken by him in Mesopotamia;"

Augustine of Hippo (354-430)

We will end this chapter with the most influential Western Church Father, St. Augustine (354-430). As is evident below, St. Augustine did not identify Mary with the Church but rather presented Mary and the Church as similar, parallel realities.

> Why is Mary the Mother of the Christ? Is it not because she has given birth to Christ's members? You to whom I am speaking are Christ's members: Who gave birth to you? I can hear your heart replying: Mother Church. **This holy, venerable Mother is like (*similis*) Mary**: she too gives birth and is a virgin.[161]

Discussion Questions

1. Discuss Marian theology before the Council of Nicaea. Include the following in your response: anonymity, virgin, and the intuitions of St. Irenaeus, Clement of Alexandria, and Origen.

2. Discuss Marian theology after the Council of Nicaea. Include the following in your answer, speculation on how the Council of

---

[161] Brendan Leahy, *The Marian Profile* (New York: New City Press, 2000), 23-24. The following is cited. *Sermo Denis*, 35.

Nicaea impacted Marian theology, the Council of Ephesus, Marian typology (describe at least two types), and St. Augustine's cautious comparison of Mary to the Church.

Chapter 7

Medieval Age: Flowering of Devotions

Introduction

During the Medieval Age, Marian theology continued to develop. Unlike St. Augustine's cautious, minimalistic Marian theology, medieval theologians identified Mary with the Church, referred to her as a Bride, a Spouse, a Queen, the Star of the Sea, and recognized her as the fulfillment of many types in the Old Testament. Along with these ways of perceiving Mary, some Medieval theologians taught that Mary was immaculate conceived and was assumed into heaven. Still other theologians from this era wrote on Mary as, through Christ, mediating grace and helping to redeem sinners. These developments were accompanied by a flowering of Marian devotions, and by Marian poetry. Two notable devotions were devotion to Mary's Seven Sorrows and the Rosary.

Identification with the Church

On Wednesday, April 22nd 2009, Benedict XVI gave a General Audience on the Frankish Benedictine

162

theologian Ambrose of Autpert (c. 730-784). "With good reason" Benedict XVI said, "Ambrose Autpert

162   https://www.museodelprado.es/en/the-collection/
online-gallery/on-line-gallery/obra/the-coronation-of-the-
virgin/, "Diego Velázquez - Coronation of the Virgin - Prado,"
photograph, https://commons.wikimedia.org/wiki/File%3ADi
ego_Vel%C3%A1zquez_-_Coronation_of_the_Virgin_-
_Prado.jpg, (accessed June 28, 2016).

is considered the first great Mariologist in the West."[163] His greatness is evident in his having anticipated St. Bernard's and Franciscan mysticism, explained the Pope, and "never deviating to disputable forms of sentimentalism" and never separating the "Mary from the mystery of the Church."[164] In addition, Ambrose, continues the Pope, "looks to Mary as a model of the Church, a model for all of us because Christ must also be born in and among us."[165]

In so doing, Ambrose began to more closely identify Mary with the Church. This identification was influenced by the Patristic age which understood the woman in Revelation, chapter twelve as representing the Church. Further developing this association of Revelation chapter twelve with the Church, Ambrose reasoned, "the Blessed and devout Virgin... daily gives birth to new peoples from which the general Body of the Mediator is formed. It is therefore not surprising if she, in whose blessed womb the Church herself deserved

[163] Benedict XVI, "Ambrose Autpert," Wed., April 22, 2009, General Audience, ewtn.com, https://www.ewtn.com/library/PAPALDOC/b16ChrstChrch79.htm, (accessed June 6, 2016).

[164] Benedict XVI, "Ambrose Autpert," Wed., April 22, 2009, General Audience, ewtn.com, https://www.ewtn.com/library/PAPALDOC/b16ChrstChrch79.htm, (accessed June 6, 2016).

[165] Benedict XVI, "Ambrose Autpert," Wed., April 22, 2009, General Audience, ewtn.com, https://www.ewtn.com/library/PAPALDOC/b16ChrstChrch79.htm, (accessed June 6, 2016).

to be united with her Head, represents the type of the Church."[166] While recognizing the relationship between Mary and the Church, Ambrose also distinguished them. In so doing he writes:

> Whether we say that it was the Mother and Virgin Mary who gave birth to Christ, or bears Christ, or say the same about the Mother and Virgin Church, in neither case do we stray from the truth of the matter. The former gave birth to the Head; the latter gave birth to the members of the Head.[167]

Saint Peter Damian (c.1007-1073) goes further than Ambrose by describing the Church as issuing forth from Mary's womb:

> Mary is a great and happy Mother, as well as a blessed Virgin, from whose womb Christ took flesh; and from Christ's flesh the Church flowed out in the water and the blood. And so in this way, and from

---

[166] Benedict XVI, "Ambrose Autpert," Wed., April 22, 2009, General Audience, ewtn.com, https://www.ewtn.com/library/PAPALDOC/b16ChrstChrch79.htm, (accessed June 6, 2016).

[167] Luigi Gambero, *Mary in the Middle Ages* (Kindle Edition: Ignatius Press, 2010), loc. 708. The following source was cited. *In Apocalypsin* V, 12, 5a; CCM 27, 450.

Mary, the Church is seen to have come forth. Each of the two is chaste; each is pure; and each is protected by the girdle of perpetual virginity.[168]

The Cistercian Isaac Stella (c. 1100-1170) even more closely relates Mary with the Church with, "Both are Mothers of Christ, but neither of the two gives birth to the whole Christ without the other."[169] Isaac Stella provides distinctions in order to understand how the two motherhoods relate to one another:

I will dwell in the Lord's inheritance" (Sir 24:11). The Lord's inheritance, in the universal sense, is the Church; in a special sense, it is Mary; in an individual sense, it is every faithful soul. Christ dwelled for nine months in the tabernacle of Mary's womb; in the tabernacle of the Church's faith, he will dwell until the final consummation of the world; and in the

---

[168] Luigi Gambero, *Mary in the Middle Ages* (Kindle Edition: Ignatius Press, 2010), loc. 1457. The following source was cited. *Sermo de sancto Joanne;* PL 144, 861B.

[169] Luigi Gambero, *Mary in the Middle Ages* (Kindle Edition: Ignatius Press, 2010), loc. 2559. The following source was cited. *Sermo 51 in Assumptione*; PL 194, 1863A; SC 339, 204.

knowledge and love of the faithful soul, he will dwell forever and ever.[170]

Bride and Spouse

Venerable Bede (c. 673-735) inserted into his *Ecclesiastical History of England* a beautiful hymn on Mary in which he refers to her as a spouse. According to Bede, this Marian hymn was "composed in elegiac verse many years ago, in praise and honor of the same queen and bride of Christ, and therefore truly a queen, because the bride of Christ...."[171] In his hymn he also calls Mary a Gate of God, Virgin Mother, Mother of Heaven's King, and bride of God.

The Frankish Benedictine Rabanus Maurus (c. 780-856) locates the bridal chamber in which God married his bride as Mary's womb. He writes, "The manner in which the Father brought about the marriage of the King, his Son, was the manner in which he associated the holy Church with himself in the mystery of the Incarnation. And that Bridegroom's bridal chamber was the womb of his Virgin

---

[170] Luigi Gambero, *Mary in the Middle Ages* (Kindle Edition: Ignatius Press, 2010), loc. 2568. The following source was cited. *Sermo 51 in Assumptione*; PL 194, 1865C; SC 339, 214-16.

[171] Venerable Bede, "Bede's Ecclesiastical History of England," trans. A.M. Sellar, chap. 20, gutenberg.org, http://www.gutenberg.org/files/38326/38326-h/38326-h.html, (accessed June 6, 2016).

Mother."[172]

The French theologian, Alain de Lille (c. 1128-1203), develops Marian bridal imagery even further by describing Mary as the spouse of Christ. Her spiritual marriage, according to Alain de Lille, took place when she gave her yes to God at the Annunciation, "He [Christ] married the Virgin, not only in a union of spirits, but also in a union of natures. And so this Incarnation is called a marriage, because it was like a kind of marital union and a joy unspeakable."[173] Alain de Lille specifically calls Christ her husband in the following excerpt, "As Bride and Mother, Mary maintained an unshakeable faithfulness toward her Husband and Son, especially in the moment of his sorrowful Passion: The disciples' faith failed, but the firmness of the Virgin's faith was not diminished."[174]

St. Albert the Great (c. 1200-1280) relates Mary as Virgin Bride to the Church by writing in his commentary on Matthew, "And so she is married (cf. Mt 1:18), so that she might stand for the

---

[172] Luigi Gambero, *Mary in the Middle Ages* (Kindle Edition: Ignatius Press, 2010), loc. 1040. The following source was cited. *Commentaria in Matthaeum* 6, 22: PL 107, 1053D.

[173] Luigi Gambero, *Mary in the Middle Ages* (Kindle Edition: Ignatius Press, 2010), loc. 2781. The following source was cited. PL 210, 77AB.

[174] Luigi Gambero, *Mary in the Middle Ages* (Kindle Edition: Ignatius Press, 2010), loc. 2781. The following source was cited. PL 210, 58B.

Church, who is Virgin and Bride."[175]

Queen

Conrad of Saxony, along with other Medieval theologians, called Mary a queen. In reference to her queenship, he writes, "They can confidently follow this queen in her kingdom if they will have followed her faithfully in this world."[176] The previously mentioned Venerable Bede describes her as a Queen Mother by relating her Motherhood of "Heaven's King" to the "honor and scepter" she received in this world which will be followed by even higher honors in heaven:[177]

> Child of a noble sire, and glorious by royal birth, more noble in her Lord's sight, the child of a noble sire. Thence **she receives queenly honor** and a scepter in this world; thence she receives honor, **awaiting higher honor above**. What need, gracious lady, to seek an earthly

---

[175] Luigi Gambero, *Mary in the Middle Ages* (Kindle Edition: Ignatius Press, 2010), loc. 3361. The following source was cited. In *Matthaeum* 1,18; Cologne, 21.1:25.

[176] Luigi Gambero, *Mary in the Middle Ages* (Kindle Edition: Ignatius Press, 2010), loc. 3184. The following source was cited. *Speculum* 1, 11, 3; Quaracchi, p. 381.

[177] Venerable Bede, "Bede's Ecclesiastical History of England," trans. A.M. Sellar, chap. 20, gutenberg.org, http://www.gutenberg.org/files/38326/38326-h/38326-h.html, (accessed June 6, 2016).

lord, even now given to the Heavenly Bridegroom?

Christ is at hand, the Bridegroom (why seek an earthly lord?) that thou mayst follow even now, methinks, in the steps of the **Mother of Heaven's King**, that thou too mayst be a mother in God. Twelve years she had **reigned**, a bride dedicated to God, then in the cloister dwelt, a bride dedicated to God. To Heaven all consecrated she lived, abounding in lofty deeds, then to Heaven all consecrated she gave up her soul.[178]

Rabanus Maurus even more directly relates Mary's Motherhood of Christ with her queensheep. "Behold, you have been lifted up above the choirs of angels, seated next to your Son the King. O happy Mother, you will reign as Queen forever. And he, to whom you offered a place to dwell in your womb, he himself has given you the kingdom of heaven."[179]

---

[178] Venerable Bede, "Bede's Ecclesiastical History of England," trans. A.M. Sellar, chap. 20, gutenberg.org, http://www.gutenberg.org/files/38326/38326-h/38326-h.html, (accessed June 6, 2016).

[179] Luigi Gambero, *Mary in the Middle Ages* (Kindle Edition: Ignatius Press, 2010), loc. 1045. The following source was cited. *In Assumptione*, PL 110, 85D.

Star of the Sea

In interpreting the meaning of Mary's name, Rabanus Maurus writes, "Because it is normal for a star to guide men to a safe haven, Mary, in this world into which Christ was born, is called Light-Bringer and Lady. Christ guides all to life, as long as they follow him, and Mary brought forth for us our true Light and Lord."[180] In agreement with this interpretation, the French bishop Fulbert of Chartres (c. 952-1028) states:

> This woman, chosen and outstanding among daughters, surely did not receive her name by pure chance or simply because it pleased her parents, as happens with most girls. No, she received her name according to a divine plan, so that the very pronouncing of her name points to something of great importance. For "Mary" means "star of the sea".[181]

---

[180] Luigi Gambero, *Mary in the Middle Ages* (Kindle Edition: Ignatius Press, 2010), loc. 1000. The following source was cited. *Homiliae in Evangelia et Epistolas* 163; PL 110, 464C. B According to Gambero, "Among the various interpretations of Mary's name, Jerome...also expresses a preference for the meaning 'star of the sea'. See *De nominibus hebraicis*; PL 23, 886."

[181] Luigi Gambero, *Mary in the Middle Ages* (Kindle Edition: Ignatius Press, 2010), loc. 1229. The following source was cited. *Sermo* 4; PL 141, 321D-322A; TMPM 3:850.

Another reason Fulbert of Chartres gives for the appropriateness of her name is as follows:

> Everyone who worships Christ, when rowing through the waves of this world, must keep his eyes fixed on this Star of the Sea; that is, on Mary. She is nearest to God, the highest pole of the universe, and they must steer the course of their life by contemplating her example. Anyone who does this will never be tossed by the wind of vainglory or broken on the shoals of adversity or drowned in the stormy whirlpool of pleasures; but he will successfully reach the safe harbor of eternal rest.[182]

Fulfillment of Old Testament Types

Along with other medieval theologians, Rabanus Maurus (c. 780-856) described Mary as fulfilling many Old Testament Types including the Woman of Genesis chapter three, verse fifteen, the burning bush of Exodus chapter three, verse 2, and Aaron's staff. With respect to the first type from Genesis, Rabanus Maurus wrote:

---

[182] Luigi Gambero, *Mary in the Middle Ages* (Kindle Edition: Ignatius Press, 2010), loc.1239. The following source was cited. *Sermo* 4; PL 141, 322AB; TMPM 3:850.

Some have understood the saying "I will put enmity between you and the woman" (Gen 3:15) as referring to the Virgin from whom the Lord was born. They understood it in this way because it was promised at that time that the Lord would be born to overthrow the enemy and destroy death, which the devil had introduced.[183]

In explaining how Mary fulfills the burning bush, Rabanus Maurus writes:

The bush, then (as some hold), is a prefiguration of the Virgin Mary, since she made the Savior blossom forth, like a rose growing out of the bush of her human body; or rather, because she brought forth the power of the divine radiance without being consumed by it. Hence we read in Exodus: "The Lord appeared to Moses in a flame of fire out of the midst of a bush; and he looked, and behold, the bush was burning, yet it

---

[183] Luigi Gambero, *Mary in the Middle Ages* (Kindle Edition: Ignatius Press, 2010), loc. 978. The following source was cited. *Commentaria in Genesim* 1, 18; PL 107, 496A.

was not consumed" (Ex 3:2).[184]

With respect to Aaron's staff, Rabanus Maurus states:

> Others think that this staff, which brought forth a flower without the presence of moisture, is the Virgin Mary, who bore the Word of God without intercourse. Of her it was written: "A shoot shall come forth from the stump of Jesse, and a flower blossom from his roots" (Is 11:1); in other words, Christ. For Christ the flower, foreshadowing his future Passion, turned purple in the white light of faith and in the red blood of his Passion. He is the flower of virgins, the crown of martyrs, the grace of those who remain chaste.[185]

Fulbert of Chartres also related Aaron's staff to Mary with:

> As that rod, without roots, without

---

[184] Luigi Gambero, *Mary in the Middle Ages* (Kindle Edition: Ignatius Press, 2010), loc. 979. The following source was cited. *De universo* 19, 6; PL 111, 513C.

[185] Luigi Gambero, *Mary in the Middle Ages* (Kindle Edition: Ignatius Press, 2010), loc. 987. The following source was cited. *Enarrationes in librum Numerorum* 2, 20; PL 108, 688B.

any natural or artificial assistance, brought forth [almond blossoms], so the Virgin Mary gave birth to the Son of God without conjugal relations. Her Son is marked out as flower and fruit: a flower, because of his beauty; a fruit, because of the benefit he brings.[186]

Isaac of Stella identifies one of the most primordial aspects of creation, the earth, as fulfilled in Mary as the New Virgin Earth. The way he makes this typology is similar to Jerome's description of how in the New Covenant all things are recapitulated, at times in the opposite order so as to reverse a curse. Along this line of reasoning, Isaac of Stella writes:[187]

There man was brought forth from earth; here God is brought forth from Mary. There, from earth still incorrupt and virgin, comes an upright man, himself a virgin; here from Mary, always incorrupt and virginal, comes the just God, himself making virgins. There, from the side

---

[186] Luigi Gambero, *Mary in the Middle Ages* (Kindle Edition: Ignatius Press, 2010), loc. 1208. The following source was cited. *Sermo* 4; PL 141, 321C; TMPM 3:849-50.

[187] Tim Staples, *Behold Your Mother: A Biblical and Historical Defense of the Marian Doctrines* (El Cajon: Catholic Answers, Kindle Edition, 2014,) loc. 1217 of 6088.

of the man, woman was created without a woman [to act as mother]; here, from a woman's womb, a man is generated without a man [to act as father]. There, from the rib of a sleeping man, a woman is built up to be a helpmate; here, from the side of the dying Christ, a Bride is consecrated. There, flesh is supplied in place of the rib [that was taken]; here, in exchange for the power that is given, weakness is assumed. There, we see two in one flesh; here, there are no longer two but one in one spirit.[188]

Immaculate Conception

In a subsequent chapter, the 1854 dogmatic definition of the Immaculate Conception by Pope Pius IX in his papal bull *Ineffabilis Deus* will be discussed. In this section, a few medieval views on Mary's Immaculate Conception will be presented. It is important to remember when reading this section that medieval theologians who argued against Mary's being immaculately conceived did so prior to the dogma of the Immaculate Conception being

---

[188] Luigi Gambero, *Mary in the Middle Ages* (Kindle Edition: Ignatius Press, 2010), loc. 2542. The following source was cited. *Sermo 54 in Nativitate;* PL 194, 1873CD; SC 339, 252-54.

clearly defined by the Church in 1854.

Eadmer of Canterbury (c. 1060-c.1126) argued in favor of Mary being conceived without sin. In doing so he writes:

> If Jeremiah was sanctified in his mother's womb because he was to be a prophet among the Gentiles, and if John, who was to go before the Lord in the spirit and power of Elijah, was filled with the Holy Spirit from his mother's womb, who will dare to say that the one and only mercy seat of the whole world, the most sweet couch of the Son of God Almighty, was deprived of the illumination of the grace of the Holy Spirit from the first instant of her conception?[189]

In demonstrating the reasonableness of his argument, Eadmer of Canterbury used an analogy based on a chestnut. He argues:

> If God allows the chestnut to be conceived, to grow, and to be formed amid spines without being punctured by them, could he not grant to a human [body], which he prepared for himself as a temple in which he

---

[189] Luigi Gambero, *Mary in the Middle Ages* (Kindle Edition: Ignatius Press, 2010), loc. 1695. The following source was cited. *De conceptione*; PL 159, 305A; Thurston-Slater, p. 9.

might dwell bodily and from which he would come forth as the perfect man in the unity of his Person, that, though this body be conceived among the spines of sins, it would nevertheless be completely un-harmed by their sharp points? He certainly could do it, and he wanted to do it. Therefore, if he wanted to do it, he did it. And now, O most blessed among women, it is clear that everything worthy that God wanted for someone other than himself, he wanted for you.[190]

Eadmer of Canterbury helped to prepare for the "subtle argumentation" of Blessed Duns Scotus (c. 1266-1308). The Subtle Doctor's argument for the Immaculate Conception is given below. In it Duns Scotus argues that Mary's preservation from original sin is the most perfect act of mediation that Christ did for anyone:

[Mary] did not contract original sin because of the excellence of her Son, inasmuch as he is Redeemer,

---

[190] Luigi Gambero, *Mary in the Middle Ages* (Kindle Edition: Ignatius Press, 2010), loc. 1703. The following source was cited. *De conception*; PL 159, 305C-306A; Thurston-Slater, p. 11.

Reconciler, and Mediator. For the most perfect mediator would perform the most perfect act of mediation on behalf of any person for whom he mediated. But Christ is the most perfect Mediator. Therefore, Christ showed the most perfect possible degree of mediating with respect to any creature or person whose Mediator he was. But for no other person did he exhibit a more excellent degree of mediation than he did for Mary. . . . But this would not have happened if he had not merited that she should be preserved from original sin. I prove this with three arguments. First, in reference to God, to whom Christ reconciles others; second, in reference to evil, from which he liberates others; third, in reference to the debt of the person whom he reconciles to God. First. No one placates another in the highest or most perfect way for an offense that someone might commit except by preventing him from being offended. For, if he placates someone who has already been offended, so that the offended party remits [punishment], he does not placate perfectly. . . . Therefore, Christ does not perfectly placate the Trinity for the guilt to be contracted by the sons of Adam if he does not prevent the Trinity from being offended by at least someone, so that consequently the soul of some one descendant of Adam would not have this guilt. Second. The most perfect Mediator merits the removal of all punishment from the one whom he reconciles. But the original fault is a greater punishment than even the loss of the vision of God . . . because, of all punishments that might befall the intellectual nature, sin is the greatest. Therefore, if Christ reconciled in the most perfect way possible, he merited to remove that most heavy punishment from [at least] someone—and this could only be his Mother. Further, it seems that Christ restored and reconciled us from original sin more directly than from actual sin, because the necessity of the Incarnation, Passion, and so forth, is commonly attributed to original sin, but it is commonly supposed that he was a perfect Mediator with respect to [at least] one person; for example, Mary, given that he preserved her from all actual sin. Therefore, he acted similarly on her behalf and preserved her from original sin. . . . Third. A person who has been reconciled is not indebted in the greatest possible way to his mediator unless he has received the greatest possible good from him. But that innocence, which is the preservation from contracting or needing to contract guilt, can be had by means of a mediator. Therefore, no person would be indebted in the highest possible way to Christ as his Mediator if Christ had not preserved someone from original sin.[191]

In contrast with Duns Scotus, St. Thomas Aquinas argues that Mary was not free from original sin since if she were she would not have needed the redemption of Christ which is contrary to Scripture (1 Timothy 4:10):

The sanctification of the Blessed Virgin cannot be understood as having taken place before animation, for two reasons. First, because the sanctification of which we are speaking, is nothing but the cleansing from original sin: for

---

[191] Luigi Gambero, *Mary in the Middle Ages* (Kindle Edition: Ignatius Press, 2010), loc. 3656. The following source was cited. In 3 *Sententiarum*, d. 3, q. 1; ed. Mariani, pp. 181-84.

sanctification is a "perfect cleansing," as Dionysius says (Div. Nom. xii). Now sin cannot be taken away except by grace, the subject of which is the rational creature alone. Therefore before the infusion of the rational soul, the Blessed Virgin was not sanctified.

Secondly, because, since the rational creature alone can be the subject of sin; before the infusion of the rational soul, the offspring conceived is not liable to sin. And thus, in whatever manner the Blessed Virgin would have been sanctified before animation, she could never have incurred the stain of original sin: and thus she would not have needed redemption and salvation which is by Christ, of whom it is written (Matthew 1:21): "He shall save His people from their sins." But this is unfitting, through implying that Christ is not the "Savior of all men," as He is called (1 Timothy 4:10). It remains, therefore, that the Blessed Virgin was sanctified after animation.[192]

Assumption

As was evident in the previous chapter, the Patristic age focused on two of the four Marian doctrines. The two which the Church Fathers emphasized are the Perpetual Virginity of Mary and Mary as Mother of God. During the Medieval Age, these two doctrines along with two others were extensively written about. The latter two doctrines, though, would only be clearly defined many centuries later. We just covered Mary being immaculately conceived. We will now look at how medieval theologians reflected on Mary's Assumption into heaven.

Early in the Medieval age, Ambrose Autpert (c. 730-784) refers to a liturgical celebration on Mary's Assumption into heaven. He writes:

> Dearly beloved brethren, a day most worthy of honor has arrived, surpassing the feast days of all the saints. Today, I say, is a glorious day, a day of fame, a day in which the Virgin Mary is believed to have passed from this world. And so all the earth, made splendid by the passing of so great a Virgin, sings

---

[192] Thomas Aquinas, "Summa Theologica," III, q. 27, a. 2, corpus, newadvent.org, http://www.newadvent.org/summa/4027.htm#article1, (accessed June 8, 2016).

praises with the greatest exultation.[193]

Other Medieval theologians who refer to Mary's Assumption into heaven include St. Paschasius Radbertus (785-865), St. Bernard of Clairvaux (1090-1153), and St. Bernardino of Siena (1380-1444).

Paschasius Radbertus in referring to Mary's Assumption exclaims:

> Today, the glorious and ever-virgin Mary has gone up into the heavens. Rejoice, I beg you, because she has been lifted up (if I may say it) in a way beyond words and reigns forever with Christ. Today, the Queen of the world is taken away from the earth and from this present worthless world. Again I say, rejoice! For she, sure of her incorruptible glory, has now arrived at the heavenly palace.[194]

Along with Ambrose Autpert and

---

[193] Luigi Gambero, *Mary in the Middle Ages* (Kindle Edition: Ignatius Press, 2010), loc. 676. The following source was cited. *De Assumptione sanctae Mariae* 1; PL 39, 2130; CCM 27/B, 1027.

[194] Luigi Gambero, *Mary in the Middle Ages* (Kindle Edition: Ignatius Press, 2010), loc. 1140. The following source was cited. *Cogitis me*, 4; PL 30, 126B; Ripberger 23, pp. 67-68.

Paschasius Radbertus, St. Bernard of Clairvaux also refers to the Church celebrating Mary's Assumption into heaven:

> I have learned from the Church to celebrate with the greatest veneration this day, on which the Virgin, taken up from the wicked world, caused the most splendid and joyful festival in heaven.[195]

Since St. Bernardine of Siena wrote so clearly and extensively on Mary's Assumption into heaven he has been referred to as the Doctor of the Assumption.[196] Pope Pius XII in his 1950 Apostolic Constitution *Munificentissiums Deus*, in which he defines the Dogma of the Assumption, summarizes the Doctor of the Assumption's teaching as follows:

> In the fifteenth century, during a later period of scholastic theology, St. Bernardine of Siena collected and diligently evaluated all that the medieval theologians had said and taught on this question. He was not

---

[195] Luigi Gambero, *Mary in the Middle Ages* (Kindle Edition: Ignatius Press, 2010), loc. 2022. The following source was cited. *Sermo 1 in Assumptione* 1; PL 183, 415.

[196] Luigi Gambero, *Mary in the Middle Ages* (Kindle Edition: Ignatius Press, 2010), loc. 4271.

content with setting down the principal considerations which these writers of an earlier day had already expressed, but he added others of his own. The likeness between God's Mother and her divine Son, in the way of the nobility and dignity of body and of soul - a likeness that forbids us to think of the heavenly Queen as being separated from the heavenly King - makes it entirely imperative that Mary "should be only where Christ is." Moreover, it is reasonable and fitting that not only the soul and body of a man, but also the soul and body of a woman should have obtained heavenly glory. Finally, since the Church has never looked for the bodily relics of the Blessed Virgin nor proposed them for the veneration of the people, we have a proof on the order of a sensible experience.[197]

---

[197] Pius XII, "Apostolic Constitution of Pope Pius XII, Munificentissimus Deus," November 1, 1950, no. 33, w2.vatican.va, http://w2.vatican.va/content/pius-xii/en/apost_constitutions/documents/hf_p-xii_apc_19501101_munificentissimus-deus.html, (accessed June 8, 2016).

Mediating Redemption

Mary's subordinate role as mediator was a theme that recurred throughout the Medieval Age. The following are a few excerpts from key theologians on Mary's role as mediatrix in a way that is always second to her son, the one mediator. St. Bonaventure in referring to her auxiliary role in Christ's mediation writes the following:

> Eve expels us from paradise and sells us [into the slavery of sin], but Mary brings us back and buys our freedom.[198]

> Mary, the strong and faithful woman, paid this price, since when Christ suffered on the Cross to pay this price to redeem us, the blessed Virgin was present, accepting God's will and consenting to it.[199]

> Those who are rooted in the Virgin Mother with love and devotion are

---

[198] Luigi Gambero, *Mary in the Middle Ages* (Kindle Edition: Ignatius Press, 2010), loc. 3075. The following source was cited. *De donis Spiritus Sancti*, collectio 6, 14; Quaracchi, 5:486.

[199] Luigi Gambero, *Mary in the Middle Ages* (Kindle Edition: Ignatius Press, 2010), loc. 3078. The following source was cited. *De donis Spiritus Sancti*, collectio 6, 15; Quaracchi, 5:486.

sanctified by her, because she asks her Son to give it to them.[200]

In line with his earlier brother Franciscan Bonaventure, Saint Bernardino of Siena likewise refers to Mary's role as mediator granted to her by Christ:

> The conception of the Son of God conferred upon the Blessed Virgin the right to administrate and govern everything that was granted to the Son.[201]

> From the moment when she conceived God in her womb, she had—if I may be allowed the expression—a certain jurisdiction and authority over all the temporal processions of the Holy Spirit, so that no creature receives any grace of virtue except through the distribution of that grace by the Virgin Mary.

---

[200] Luigi Gambero, *Mary in the Middle Ages* (Kindle Edition: Ignatius Press, 2010), loc. 3084. The following source was cited. *Sermo de Purificatione* 2; Quaracchi, 9:646.

[201] Luigi Gambero, *Mary in the Middle Ages* (Kindle Edition: Ignatius Press, 2010), loc. 4291. The following source was cited. *De gratia et gloria beatae Virginia*, sermon 61, a. 1, c. 7; Opera omnia, 2:377.

In the fifteenth century, Antoninus of Florence explicitly calls Mary a Mediatrix with:

> She has been made the middle term, or Mediatrix, between God and men, for which reason the Church sings: "Mediatrix of men, washer-away of offenses, forgiveness of sins", because she obtains these things. And so sinners, who have become rivals and enemies of God by their offenses, should have recourse . . . to this Mediatrix, in order to be reconciled to God. For just as the lawsuit between God and men is settled by her mediation, in the same way, the cases between men and the devil are ended by her.[202]

An earlier saint, St. Bridget of Sweden (1303-1373), does not refer to Mary with the title Mediatrix in the following excerpt, but the image of a rainbow she uses well evokes Mary's role in mediation. According to St. Bridget, Mary appeared to her and said:

> I am she who hovers over the world in unceasing prayer, like the rainbow

---

[202] Luigi Gambero, *Mary in the Middle Ages* (Kindle Edition: Ignatius Press, 2010), loc. 4438. The following source was cited. *Summa Theologica*, c. 5; Verona, col. 937.

that stands above the clouds, which seems to bend down and touch the earth with its two ends. And I consider myself to be like a rainbow, because I bend down to the inhabitants of the world, touching the good ones and the bad ones with my prayer. I bend down to the good ones, to make them firm in keeping the precepts of holy Church. And I bend down to the bad ones, lest they persevere in their wickedness and become even worse.[203]

Marian Devotions

In this final section of this chapter we will glance at two popular medieval devotions to our Lady: the Seven Sorrows and the Rosary. Fr. Mitch Pacwa, S.J., in his book *Mary-Virgin, Mother and Queen* describes one popular medieval devotion to Mary called the Seven Sorrows. This devotion began around the thirteenth century. The Servite order embraced this devotion and promoted it. They promoted devotion to the Seven Sorrows by celebrating local liturgical Feasts of Mary's Seven Sorrows. Centuries later, in 1814, Pope Pius VII placed this feast on the universal calendar. One way

---

[203] Luigi Gambero, *Mary in the Middle Ages* (Kindle Edition: Ignatius Press, 2010), loc. 4059. The following source was cited. *Revelationes*, lib. 3, c. 10; ed. Durante, p. 183.

people practiced devotion to the Seven Sorrows was by praying a chaplet consisting of one Our Father and seven Hail Mary's for each sorrow of Mary. Her sorrows include:

- Simeon's prophesying that a sword will pierce Mary's heart (Lk. 2:34-35)
- The Holy Family's flight into Egypt (Mt. 2:13-15)
- The finding of the child Jesus in the Temple (Lk. 2:43-50)
- Mary seeing Jesus on His Way of the Cross
- Jesus' crucifixion and death
- Mary holds the body of Jesus in her arms (Mt. 27:57-59)
- Jesus' body is laid in the tomb (Jn. 19:40-42)[204]

The Dominican Alanus de Rupe (1428-1475) greatly contributed to establishing the second of the medieval Marian devotions which we will conclude with, the Rosary. According to the Marian scholar Luigi Gambero, Alanus de Rupe was responsible for transforming the medieval practice of praying 150 Hail Marys in three groups of fifty. Alanus de Rupe describes this manner of reciting the Rosary in his treatise *Compendium psalterii beatissimae Trinitatis*. He did so by further breaking up the 150

---

[204] Mitch Pacwa, *Mary-Virgin, Mother, and Queen: A Bible Study Guide for Catholics* (Huntington: Our Sunday Visitor Publishing, 2013), 83.

Hail Marys into ten groups of fifteen.[205]

In the prologue to the treatise, Alanus de Rupe describes the recitation of 150 Hail Marys as similar to the praying of the 150 psalms of the Divine Office. Unlike the Divine Office, though, the recitation of 150 Hail Mary's can be prayed by all, including those who cannot read.[206] Alanus claims that the Rosary did not originate during his times (the Medieval age) but rather was taught and practiced since apostolic times. The reason why this Marian devotion flourished during the medieval times was because, according to Alanus, Mary revealed to the founder of the Dominican Order, St. Dominic, a particular way to pray the Rosary, namely by meditating on the Incarnation for the first fifty Hail Marys, and then upon the Passion and Resurrection for the subsequent two fifty sets of Hail Marys.[207]

Discussion Questions

1. Compare and contrast Augustine's understanding of the Mary in relationship to the Church with how Ambrose of Autpert, Peter

---

[205] Luigi Gambero, *Mary in the Middle Ages* (Kindle Edition: Ignatius Press, 2010), loc. 4633.

[206] Luigi Gambero, *Mary in the Middle Ages* (Kindle Edition: Ignatius Press, 2010), loc. 4636.

[207] Luigi Gambero, *Mary in the Middle Ages* (Kindle Edition: Ignatius Press, 2010), loc. 4645. The practice of meditating on a mystery from Mary and Jesus life for each group of ten has been attributed to a Carthusian monk Dominic of Prussia (1382-1461).

Damian, and Isaac Stella wrote on this relationship. Do so in a specific manner for each theologian.

2. Explain, with reference to specific medieval theologians, how medieval theologians related Mary as Bride and Spouse to Mary as Queen.

3. Discuss how medieval theologians described Mary as fulfilling Old Testament types namely, as the New Virgin Earth, the Woman of Genesis chapter three, the burning bush of Exodus chapter three, and Aaron's staff.

4. Compare and contrast Eadmer of Canterbury, Duns Scotus and Thomas Aquinas on the Immaculate conception in specific ways for each theologian.

5. What reasons did Bernardine of Siena, the Doctor of the Assumption, give in arguing that Mary's Assumption is fitting?

6. How can presenting Mary as mediator be problematic? How did certain medieval theologians present her role as mediator in an orthodox manner? Discuss this in reference to specific medieval theologians.

Chapter 8

Vatican II and Post-Vatican II

Introduction

During and after the medieval era, Marian devotion was expressed at times in excessive manners. In summarizing these excesses, von Balthasar writes:

> Here we give merely a brief summary of the excesses that start as early as the late Byzantines and in the twelfth century in the West. Mary's universal intercession is heightened to a quasi-divine "omnipotence", which is hers because the Son, who was obedient to her for so long on earth, remains obedient to her in heaven. This omnipotence can even break ultimate decrees issued by the Son; it is an "almighty power of mercy" that stands over against the Son's almighty justice and wrath. The title of Theotokos leads some to conclude that, since she shares the eternal Son

with the divine Father, she herself is "divinized", even to the extent of possessing prerogatives that God himself does not have. Her substance is said to be eternal and celestial, she is said to be a co-creator of the world, together with God, "supplementing the Trinity". Particularly embarrassing is the conclusion that, since Mary is "Mistress of the universe", "Empress", and so forth, we should all bind ourselves to her as her slaves (*douloi*), her "pages", her "lackeys"—and here the earlier idea recurs—in order to attain divine grace "more quickly" through her than through her Son, who is preoccupied with justice. Such exaggerations and distortions, and many others, were the product of pious imagination; not only did they create a stumbling block, understandably, for Protestants: they were clearly getting farther and farther away from authentic Catholic tradition.[208]

Before Vatican Council II (1962-1965), von

---

[208] Hans Urs von Balthasar, *Theo-Drama: Theological Dramatic Theory: Dramatis Personae: Persons in Christ*, Vol. 3, trans. G. Harrison (San Francisco: Ignatius Press, 1992), 314.

Balthasar and other theologians attempted to return Marian devotion and theology back towards its rightful place in Catholic tradition. The essential way to do so, recommends Ratzinger, is "to keep constantly in mind its simple, christological starting point—not in order to abolish it, but in order to situate it properly."[209] In this chapter, we will study the various ways by which the Church resituated Marian theology around Christ at the center. First, the three major pre-Vatican II theological movements that directly dealt with Marian theology will be discussed. Then, we will see how these movements were present at Vatican Council II. Finally, the Marian theology of recent popes will be presented.

210

---

[209] Joseph Ratzinger, Hans Urs von Balthasar, trans. A. Walker *Mary: The Church at the Source* (San Francisco: Ignatius Press, 2005), 9.

[210] Lothar Wolleh, "Second Vatican Council by Lothar Wolleh 005.jpg," photograph, https://commons.wikimedia.org/wiki/File%3ASecond_Vatica

Pre-Vatican II and Vatican II

One major ecclesial movement that arose before the Vatican Council II was the Marian movement. The Marian movement was in part sparked by a number of the major apparitions of Mary including at La Salette, Lourdes, and Fatima. A second major pre-Vatican Council II ecclesial movement was the modern liturgical movement. The liturgical movement gained momentum during the nineteenth and twentieth century from the liturgical revival at Solesmes, France and from the liturgical renewal promoted by St. Pius X (r. 1903-1914).[211] A third major pre-Vatican Council II movement was the ecumenical movement which the Catholic Church participated in even though the movement began among Protestant Churches. One early pre-Vatican II sign of this Catholic participation is evident in the cautious December 20, 1949, instruction of the Holy Office titled, *On the "Ecumenical Movement"*.[212]

---

n_Council_by_Lothar_Wolleh_005.jpg (accessed June 28, 2016).

[211] Joseph Ratzinger, Hans Urs von Balthasar, trans. A. Walker *Mary: The Church at the Source* (San Francisco: Ignatius Press, 2005), 19-20.

[212] Holy Office, "On the 'Ecumenical Movement': An Instruction of the Holy Office," ewtn.com, https://www.ewtn.com/library/CURIA/CDFECUM.HTM, (accessed June 10, 2016). An example of the cautious approach of the Holy See in the document to the ecumenical movement is as follows. "All the aforesaid conferences and meetings, public and non-public, large and small, which are called for the purpose of affording an opportunity for the Catholic and the

In contrast with the personal, intimate, and subjective nature of the Marian movement, which was inspired by both modern private revelations and by medieval Marian spirituality, the liturgical movement stressed that it was objective, sacramental, and based primarily on public revelation as interpreted by the patristic era.[213] A certain falseness of this dichotomy between these two movements was demonstrated when after the conclusion of World War II a number of leading theologians showed how genuine Marian piety is rooted in the bible, is present in the writings of the Church Fathers, is intrinsic to the liturgy, and is

---

non-Catholic party for the sake of discussion to treat of matters of faith and morals, each presenting on even terms the doctrine of his own faith, are subject to the prescriptions of the Church which were recalled to mind in the <Monitum, "Cum compertum>," of this Congregation under date of 5 June, 1948.[6] Hence mixed congresses are not absolutely forbidden; but they are not to be held without the previous permission of the competent Ecclesiastical Authority. The <Monitum>, however, does not apply to catechetical instructions, even when given to many together, nor to conferences in which Catholic doctrine is explained to non-Catholics who are prospective converts: even though the opportunity is afforded for the non-Catholics to explain also the doctrine of their church so that they may understand clearly and thoroughly in what respect it agrees with the Catholic doctrine and in what it differs therefrom."

[213] Joseph Ratzinger, Hans Urs von Balthasar, trans. A. Walker *Mary: The Church at the Source* (San Francisco: Ignatius Press, 2005), 20.

personal.[214]

During the Council, the liturgical movement and the ecumenical movement jointly, describes Ratzinger, "opposed the Marian movement" to such an extent that "the two parties threatened to become irreconcilable alternatives."[215] The tension between these forces at the council reached a highpoint on October 29, 1963 when the Council Fathers voted on whether to present Marian theology in a separate document or to include Marian theology in the Constitution of the Church, *Lumen Gentium.*

Representing the liturgical and ecumenical movement's concerns, the Austrian Cardinal König argued that Marian theology should not stand alone in a separate document. Representing the Marian movement concerns, Cardinal Rufino Santos of Manila argued that Marian theology ought to be treated in a separate text. When the vote was taken, the position of Cardinal König was favored, but by a small margin. The vote, reports Ratzinger, who was a theological consultant at the council, was "1114 to

---

[214] Joseph Ratzinger, Hans Urs von Balthasar, trans. A. Walker *Mary: The Church at the Source* (San Francisco: Ignatius Press, 2005), 22-23. The theologians whom Ratzinger refers to are "Hugo Rahner, A. Müller, K. Delahaye, R. Laurentin, and O. Semmelroth."

[215] Joseph Ratzinger, Hans Urs von Balthasar, trans. A. Walker *Mary: The Church at the Source* (San Francisco: Ignatius Press, 2005), 17.

1074".[216] Consequently, Marian theology was incur-
porated into *Lumen Gentium* in chapter eight
entitled, *The Blessed Virgin Mary, Mother of God
in the Mystery of Christ and the Church*. In
affirming all four Marian doctrines, number fifty-
nine of chapter eight reads:

> But since it has pleased God not to
> manifest solemnly the mystery of the
> salvation of the human race before
> He would pour forth the Spirit
> promised by Christ, we see the
> apostles before the day of Pentecost
> "persevering with one mind in
> prayer with the women and Mary the
> Mother of Jesus, and with His
> brethren", and Mary by her prayers
> imploring the gift of the Spirit, who
> had already overshadowed her in the
> Annunciation. Finally, the Immacu-
> late Virgin, preserved free from all
> guilt of original sin, on the com-
> pletion of her earthly sojourn, was
> taken up body and soul into
> heavenly glory, and exalted by the
> Lord as Queen of the universe, that
> she might be the more fully
> conformed to her Son, the Lord of

---

[216] Joseph Ratzinger, Hans Urs von Balthasar, trans. A.
Walker *Mary: The Church at the Source* (San Francisco:
Ignatius Press, 2005), 22.

lords and the conqueror of sin and death.[217]

Of the four Marian doctrines, the one that is most prominent throughout chapter eight is Mary as Mother of God. Her motherhood is clearly and carefully presented in relationship to Christ, as the "one Mediator"[218] and to the Church. In number sixty, Mary's "subordinate role"[219] in mediating graces is described as follows:

> There is but one Mediator as we know from the words of the apostle, "for there is one God and one mediator of God and men, the man Christ Jesus, who gave himself a redemption for all". The maternal duty of Mary toward men in no wise obscures or diminishes this unique mediation of Christ, but rather shows His power. For all the salvific

---

[217] Vatican Council II, "Lumen Gentium," no. 59, Vatican.va, http://www.vatican.va/archive/hist_councils/ii_vatican_council/documents/vat-ii_const_19641121_lumen-gentium_en.html, (accessed May 16, 2016).

[218] Vatican Council II, "Lumen Gentium," no. 60, Vatican.va, http://www.vatican.va/archive/hist_councils/ii_vatican_council/documents/vat-ii_const_19641121_lumen-gentium_en.html, (accessed May 16, 2016).

[219] Vatican Council II, "Lumen Gentium," no. 62, Vatican.va, http://www.vatican.va/archive/hist_councils/ii_vatican_council/documents/vat-ii_const_19641121_lumen-gentium_en.html, (accessed May 16, 2016).

influence of the Blessed Virgin on men originates, not from some inner necessity, but from the divine pleasure. It flows forth from the superabundance of the merits of Christ, rests on His mediation, depends entirely on it and draws all its power from it. In no way does it impede, but rather does it foster the immediate union of the faithful with Christ.[220]

When referring to the various exalted titles of Mary, number sixty-two once again makes certain that these are understood in light of Christ as the "one Mediator":

This maternity of Mary in the order of grace began with the consent which she gave in faith at the Annunciation and which she sustained without wavering beneath the cross, and lasts until the eternal fulfillment of all the elect. Taken up to heaven she did not lay aside this salvific duty, but by her constant

---

[220] Vatican Council II, "Lumen Gentium," no. 60, Vatican.va, http://www.vatican.va/archive/hist_councils/ii_vatican_coun cil/documents/vat-ii_const_19641121_lumen-gentium_en.html, (accessed May 16, 2016).

Fr. Peter Samuel Kucer, MSA

intercession continued to bring us
the gifts of eternal salvation. By her
maternal charity, she cares for the
brethren of her Son, who still
journey on earth surrounded by
dangers and cultics, until they are
led into the happiness of their true
home. Therefore the Blessed Virgin
is invoked by the Church under the
titles of Advocate, Auxiliatrix,
Adjutrix, and Mediatrix. This,
however, is to be so understood that
it neither takes away from nor adds
anything to the dignity and
efficaciousness of Christ the one
Mediator.[221]

Von Balthasar points out that not only is the
Marian principle of the Church located by Vatican
II docu-ments within the communion of the
Church, but the Petrine Principle (the office of the
papacy) is also situated within the communion of
the Church and not isolated from the Church.[222]
This is evident in Vatican II's *Decree On the
Pastoral Office of Bishops*. This decree

---

[221] Vatican Council II, "Lumen Gentium," no. 62,
Vatican.va,
http://www.vatican.va/archive/hist_councils/ii_vatican_coun
cil/documents/vat-ii_const_19641121_lumen-
gentium_en.html, (accessed May 16, 2016).
[222] Brendan Leahy, *The Marian Profile* (New York: New
City Press, 2000), 35.

acknowledges that bishops have authority by virtue of their office. In other words, episcopal authority is not merely delegated to them by the pope. Number four of the decree reads, "The bishops, by virtue of their sacramental consecration and their hierarchical communion with the head of the college and its other members, are constituted members of the episcopal body."[223] Similarly, *Lumen Gentium* explains that bishops are not "to be regarded as vicars of the Roman Pontiff; for they exercise the power which they possess in their own right and are called in the truest sense of the term prelates of the people whom they govern."[224]

These two dimensions of the Church, the Petrine and the Marian, asserts von Balthasar, were well described by Vatican II documents since they are presented within the communion of the Church and the roles are described as complementary. The Petrine, structural and hierarchical dimension externally and objectively unites the Church while the Marian principle unites the church more

---

[223] Second Vatican Council, Decree on the Pastoral Office of Bishops in the Church, *Christus Dominus,* no. 4 (28 October 1965), in Vatican Council II: The Conciliar and Post Conciliar Documents, ed. Austin Flannery (Boston: Daughters of St. Paul, 1980), 565-566.

[224] Second Vatican Council, Dogmatic Constitution on the Church, *Lumen Gentium,* no. 27 (21 November 1964), in Vatican Council II: The Conciliar and Post Conciliar Documents, ed. Austin Flannery (Boston: Daughters of St. Paul, 1980), 283.

intimately, internally, and subjectively.[225] The objective (Petrine, liturgical, public revelation) and the subjective (Marian, devotional, subjective holiness, private revelation) are, insists von Balthasar, to be in harmony with one another in the Church. When this harmony occurs, he states, "the result is a Christian life that the Church can hold up, can 'canonize', as exemplary and worthy of imitation, in as much as it reflects the splendor of the holiness of God and Christ."[226]

The biblical scholar Brant Pitre's comments on marriage can help to understand the importance of balancing the objective and subjective dimensions of the Church. In reference to marriage, Brant Pitre states "that a headless person is a dead person and a heartless person is a dead person. The question is the head or heart more important is meaningless since they both need each other in an essential way. The man is naturally ordered to governing, and the woman is naturally ordered to loving. The end is peace and harmony at home."[227] Similarly, but with a difference, the subjective, Marian "holiness of the heart" dimension of the Church and the "objective holiness of the structure," Petrine dimension of the

---

[225] Brendan Leahy, *The Marian Profile* (New York: New City Press, 2000), 35-38.

[226] Joseph Ratzinger, Hans Urs von Balthasar, trans. A. Walker *Mary: The Church at the Source* (San Francisco: Ignatius Press, 2005), 136-137.

[227] Possibly not a direct quote, but very nearly so. Brant Pitre, *Jesus the Bridegroom: The Divine Love Story in the Bible,* CD 15 of 20 (Catholic Productions).

Church need each other.[228] These two dimensions of the Catholic Church are intended by God, further explains von Balthasar, to "interpenetrate and complement each other. ... Mariology and the doctrine of office are not side chapels of Catholic dogmatics; rather, they are central, integrating aspects of ecclesial catholicity."[229]

Modern Papacy

In this final section of the chapter, we will glance at four modern popes who have complemented one another with their different Marian perspectives: Paul VI, John Paul II, Benedict XVI, and Francis. The Marian scholar Antoine Nachef categorizes the first two popes by naming Paul VI's approach as "existential" and John Paul II style as "personalist."[230] The next two popes' approaches can be described as developmental, for Benedict XVI, and devotional, for Francis.

---

[228] Joseph Ratzinger, Hans Urs von Balthasar, trans. A. Walker *Mary: The Church at the Source* (San Francisco: Ignatius Press, 2005), 172-174.

[229] Joseph Ratzinger, Hans Urs von Balthasar, trans. A. Walker *Mary: The Church at the Source* (San Francisco: Ignatius Press, 2005), 174.

[230] Antoine Nachef, *Mary's Pope: John Paul II, Mary, and the Church Since Vatican II* (Franklin: Sheed & Ward, 2000), 2.

Paul VI

On December 7, 1965, at the close of Vatican Council II, Pope Paul VI formally called Mary "Mother of the Church."[231] In 1974, his existential, or practical, contribution to Marian theology was made particularly manifest in his Apostolic Exhortation *Marialis Cultus*. In the exhortation, the Holy Father instructs how the Church is to liturgically and devotionally celebrate Marian theology. The exhortation is divided into three parts.

The first part, entitled "Devotion to the Blessed Virgin Mary in the Liturgy," describes the ways by which the Church may venerate Mary in the Revised Roman Liturgy. This first part includes a section on Mary as the "Model of the Church in Divine Worship."

---

[231] Paul VI, "Address of Pope Paul VI During the Last General Meeting of the Second Vatican Council", December 7, 1965, w2.vatican.va, http://w2.vatican.va/content/paul-vi/en/speeches/1965/documents/hf_p-vi_spe_19651207_epilogo-concilio.html, (accessed June 10, 2016). "[W]e again invoke the intercession of St. John the Baptist and of St. Joseph, who are the patrons of the ecumenical council; of the holy Apostles Peter and Paul, the foundations and columns of the Holy Church; and with them of St. Ambrose, the bishop whose feast we celebrate today, as it were uniting in him the Church of the East and of the West. We also earnestly implore the protection of the most Blessed Mary, the Mother of Christ and therefore called by us also Mother of the Church. With one voice and with one heart we give thanks and glory to the living and true God, to the one and sovereign God, to the Father, to the Son and to the Holy Spirit. Amen."

The second part, entitled "The Renewal of Devotion to Mary," first describes "Trinitarian, Christological, and Ecclesial Aspects of Devotion to the Blessed Virgin." Then, in section two, the Holy Father goes through "Four Guidelines for Devotion to the Blessed Virgin: Biblical, Liturgical, Ecumenical, and Anthropological."[232] In this second section of part two, the pope cautions against "certain attitudes of piety which are incorrect."[233] Such attitudes include, "the exaggeration of content and form which even falsifies doctrine and likewise the small-mindedness which obscures the figure and mission of Mary ... vain credulity, which substitutes reliance on merely external practices for serious commitment .... [and] sterile and ephemeral sentimentality, so alien to the spirit of the Gospel that demands persevering and practical action."[234]

The third part, entitled "Observations on Two

---

[232] Paul VI, "Marialis Cultus," February 2, 1974, no. 29, w2.vatican.va, http://w2.vatican.va/content/paul-vi/en/apost_exhortations/documents/hf_p-vi_exh_19740202_marialis-cultus.html, (accessed June 10, 2016).

[233] Paul VI, "Marialis Cultus," February 2, 1974, no. 38, w2.vatican.va, http://w2.vatican.va/content/paul-vi/en/apost_exhortations/documents/hf_p-vi_exh_19740202_marialis-cultus.html, (accessed June 10, 2016).

[234] Paul VI, "Marialis Cultus," February 2, 1974, no. 38, w2.vatican.va, http://w2.vatican.va/content/paul-vi/en/apost_exhortations/documents/hf_p-vi_exh_19740202_marialis-cultus.html, (accessed June 10, 2016).

Exercises of Piety: The Angelus and the Rosary," encourages the praying of the Angelus and the Rosary. With respect to the rosary, the pope strongly recommends "the recitation of the family Rosary"[235] which "should be considered as one of the best and most efficacious prayers in common that the Christian family is invited to recite."[236]

John Paul II

Even though John Paul II dedicated himself to Mary with his episcopal motto *Totus Tuus* (All Yours),[237] he once distanced himself from Marian

---

[235] Paul VI, "Marialis Cultus," February 2, 1974, no. 52, w2.vatican.va, http://w2.vatican.va/content/paul-vi/en/apost_exhortations/documents/hf_p-vi_exh_19740202_marialis-cultus.html, (accessed June 10, 2016).

[236] Paul VI, "Marialis Cultus," February 2, 1974, no. 54, w2.vatican.va, http://w2.vatican.va/content/paul-vi/en/apost_exhortations/documents/hf_p-vi_exh_19740202_marialis-cultus.html, (accessed June 10, 2016).

[237] John Paul II, "Rosarium Virginis Mariae," no. 15, October 16, 2002, ewtn.com, http://www.ewtn.com/library/papaldoc/jp2rosar.htm, (accessed June 10, 2016). "This role of Mary, totally grounded in that of Christ and radically subordinated to it, "in no way obscures or diminishes the unique mediation of Christ, but rather shows its power".[20] This is the luminous principle expressed by the Second Vatican Council which I have so powerfully experienced in my own life and have made the basis of my episcopal motto: *Totus Tuus*. The motto is of course inspired by the teaching of Saint Louis Marie Grignion de Montfort, who explained in the following words Mary's role in the process of our configuration to Christ:

devotion. He explains this in *Crossing the Threshold of Hope*:

> During the Second World War, while I was employed as a factory worker, I came to be attracted to Marian devotion. At first, it had seemed to me that I should distance myself a bit from the Marian devotion of my childhood, in order to focus more on Christ. Thanks to Saint Louis of Montfort, I came to understand that true devotion to the Mother of God is actually Christocentric, indeed, it is very profoundly rooted in the mystery of the Blessed Trinity, and the mysteries of the Incarnation and Redemption.[238]

"Our entire perfection consists in being conformed, united and consecrated to Jesus Christ. Hence the most perfect of all devotions is undoubtedly that which conforms, unites and consecrates us most perfectly to Jesus Christ. Now, since Mary is of all creatures the one most conformed to Jesus Christ, it follows that among all devotions that which most consecrates and conforms a soul to our Lord is devotion to Mary, his Holy Mother, and that the more a soul is consecrated to her the more will it be consecrated to Jesus Christ". Never as in the Rosary do the life of Jesus and that of Mary appear so deeply joined. Mary lives only in Christ and for Christ!"

[238] Antoine Nachef, *Mary's Pope: John Paul II, Mary, and the Church Since Vatican II* (Franklin: Sheed & Ward, 2000), 7. From *Crossing the Threshold of Hope.*

The mature form of devotion to the Mother of God has stayed with me over the years, bearing fruit in the encyclicals *Redemptoris Mater* and *Mulieris Dignitatem*.[239]

An example, among many, of John Paul II's application of his philosophical personalism to Marian theology is in number forty-five of *Redemptoris Mater*:

> Of the essence of motherhood is the fact that it concerns the person. Motherhood always establishes a unique and unrepeatable relationship between two people: between mother and child and between child and mother. Even when the same woman is the mother of many children, her personal relationship with each one of them is of the very essence of motherhood. For each child is generated in a unique and unrepeatable way, and this is true both for the mother and for the child. Each child is surrounded in the same way by that maternal love on which are based the child's development and coming to matur-

---

[239] Antoine Nachef, *Mary's Pope: John Paul II, Mary, and the Church Since Vatican II* (Franklin: Sheed & Ward, 2000), 14. From *Crossing the Threshold of Hope*.

ity as a human being.

John Paul II applies his personalistic under-standing of motherhood to Mary when he describes Mary as providing an interior space free from evil in which God could fill "with every spiritual blessings."[240] In so doing, Mary established an intimate personal relationship with God and the Church as Mother of God and Mother of the Church:

> [I]n Mary's faith, first at the Annunciation and then fully at the foot of the Cross, an interior space was reopened within humanity which the eternal Father can fill "with every spiritual blessing." It is the space "of the new and eternal Covenant," and it continues to exist in the Church, which in Christ is "a kind of sacrament or sign of intimate union with God, and of the unity of all mankind."[241]

---

[240] Antoine Nachef, *Mary's Pope: John Paul II, Mary, and the Church Since Vatican II* (Franklin: Sheed & Ward, 2000), 93.

[241] John Paul II, "Redemptoris Mater," no. 28, w2.vatican.va, http://w2.vatican.va/content/john-paul-ii/en/encyclicals/documents/hf_jp-ii_enc_25031987_redemptoris-mater.html, (accessed May 15, 2016).

While John Paul II repeatedly emphasizes Mary's Motherhood and, consequently, her maternal mediation, first evident in providing a sinless interior space for God to fill, the Pope always describes her mediation from the primary Christological perspective.[242] In summarizing the

---

[242] John Paul II, "Redemptoris Mater," no. 22, w2.vatican.va, http://w2.vatican.va/content/john-paul-ii/en/encyclicals/documents/hf_jp-ii_enc_25031987_redemptoris-mater.html, (accessed June 10, 2016). "We can therefore say that in this passage of John's Gospel we find as it were a first manifestation of the truth concerning Mary's maternal care. This truth has also found expression in the teaching of the Second Vatican Council. It is important to note how the Council illustrates Mary's maternal role as it relates to the mediation of Christ. Thus we read: "Mary's maternal function towards mankind in no way obscures or diminishes the unique mediation of Christ, but rather shows its efficacy," because "there is one mediator between God and men, the man Christ Jesus" (1 Tim. 2:5). This maternal role of Mary flows, according to God's good pleasure, "from the superabundance of the merits of Christ; it is founded on his mediation, absolutely depends on it, and draws all its efficacy from it." It is precisely in this sense that the episode at Cana in Galilee offers us a sort of first announcement of Mary's mediation, wholly oriented towards Christ and tending to the revelation of his salvific power. From the text of John it is evident that it is a mediation which is maternal. As the Council proclaims: Mary became "a mother to us in the order of grace." This motherhood in the order of grace flows from her divine motherhood. Because she was, by the design of divine Providence, the mother who nourished the divine Redeemer, Mary became "an associate of unique nobility, and the Lord's humble handmaid," who "cooperated by her obedience, faith, hope and burning charity in the Savior's work of restoring supernatural life to souls." And "this maternity of Mary in the

balance struck by John Paul between Mary's subordinate mediation and Christ as the one mediator, Antoine Nachef pithly writes, "One should keep in mind that the Christological dimension of Mary's maternal mediation maintains a balance in the theology of Pope John Paul II. This means that the person and action of Mary are not swallowed up by the person and action of Christ. In turn, the person and action of Mary, although authentic and necessary, draw their necessity from the action of the Son, not from themselves."[243]

Benedict XVI

Both as a theologian and as a Pope, Benedict XVI has repeatedly written from the standpoint of a hermeneutics of continuity. What this essentially means is that the Holy Spirit, whom God the Father sent into his Church after His Son ascended into heaven, is an abiding spirit whose love is constant and continuous and not one characterized by rupture and discontinuity. For this reason, Ratzinger interprets every ecumenical council, including Vatican Council II, as not as occasions of rupture but rather in continuity with tradition, with the

---

order of grace. . .will last without interruption until the eternal fulfillment of all the elect.""

[243] Antoine Nachef, *Mary's Pope: John Paul II, Mary, and the Church Since Vatican II* (Franklin: Sheed & Ward, 2000), 152-153.

past.[244] In his 1985 interview with Vittorio Messori, he explained:

> This schematism of a *before* and *after* in the history of the Church, wholly unjustified by the documents of Vatican II, which do nothing but reaffirm the continuity of Catholicism, must be decidedly opposed. There is no 'pre-' or 'post-' conciliar Church: there is but one, unique Church that walks the path toward the Lord, ever deepening and ever better understanding the treasure of faith that he himself has entrusted to her. There are no leaps in this history, there are no fractures, and there is no break in continuity. In no wise did the Council intend to introduce a temporal dichotomy in the Church."[245]

Similarly, in his Marian work *Daughter Zion*, Ratzinger reveals a falsely perceived dichotomy

---

[244] Ratzinger Report 35. Joseph Ratzinger, "The Holy Spirit as Communio: Concerning the Relationship of Pneumatology and Spirituality in Augustine," *Communio* 25 (Summer 1998), 328.

[245] Joseph Ratzinger, *The Ratzinger Report: An Exclusive Interview on the State of the Church*, trans. Salvator Attanasio and Graham Harrison (San Francisco: Ignatius Press, 1985), 35.

between the Church's Marian devotions and Church doctrine. In describing this, he states:

> A discriminating observer of the Church's life today will discover a peculiar dichotomy in the Church's Marian belief and devotion. On the one hand, the impression is given that Mariology is a scaled-down duplicate of Christology that somehow arose on irrational grounds; or even more, it appears to be but the echo of ancient models found in the history of religions, which ineradicably returns to claim its position and value even in Christianity, although closer examination shows that there are neither historical nor theological grounds to support it. ...Indeed, many find no embarrassment in identifying the non-Christian origin of Marian belief and devotion: from Egyptian myths, from the cult of the Great Mother, from Diana of Ephesus, who, entirely on her own, became "Mother of God" (θεοτόκος) at the council convened in Ephesus.... On the other hand, there are those who plead for a magnanimity with regard to diverse types of piety: without

puritanical tendencies, we should just leave the Romans their madonnas. Behind this generosity can be seen an attitude which becomes noticeably stronger as a result of the trend toward the rationalization of Christianity: namely, the longing for a response in the religious sphere to the demands of emotion; and after that, the longing for the image of woman as virgin and mother to have a place in religion as well. Of course, mere tolerance in the face of manifold customs will not suffice to justify Marian piety. If its basis is as negligible as might appear from the considerations just mentioned, then the continued cultivation of Marian piety would be nothing but a custom contrary to truth. Such customs either wither away because their root, the truth, has dried up, or they continue to proliferate contrary to conviction, and thus destroy the correlation between truth and life. They thereby lead to a poisoning of the intellectual-spiritual organism, the results of which are incalculable.[246]

---

[246] Joseph Ratzinger, *Daughter Zion: Meditations on the*

After presenting the above perceived false dichotomies, Ratzinger, beginning with the Old Testament, systematically defends genuine Marian devotion and theology by showing how it has continuously developed in an organically, inspired manner. In a book he coauthored with von Balthasar, Ratzinger cautions against an approach to Marian devotion and theology, and by extension to all theology, that he calls an "archeological mentality." According to those who think according to this mindset, what is chronologically closest to the time of Christ is superior in all ways to what is closer to the present age. This mentality is based upon a

> model of decline: What occurs after a certain point in time appears ipso facto to be of inferior value, as if the Church were not alive and therefore capable of development in every age. As a result of all this, the kind of thinking shaped by the liturgical movement narrowed into a biblicist-positivist mentality, locked itself into a backward-looking attitude, and thus left no more room for the dynamic development of the faith. On the other hand, the distance im-

---

Church's Marian Belief, trans. J.M. McDermott (San Francisco: Ignatius Press, 1983, 9-11.

plied in historicism inevitably paved the way for "modernism"; since what is merely past is no longer living, it leaves the present isolated and so leads to self-made experimentation.[247]

Francis

Since their earliest days, Jesuits have been known for being close to the people in their missionary work. One way they connected with people was by promoting devotions. A notable example is their promotion of the Sacred Heart devotion since July 2, 1688, when in a revelation to the Visitation nun St. Margaret Mary Alacoque, the Jesuits were given the responsibility of promoting devotion to the Sacred Heart.[248]

In line with this great tradition, Pope Francis has promoted devotions. One Marian devotion he has promoted is called Mary Untier of Knots. He encountered this devotion in a deep way when making a pilgrimage to the Bavarian city of Augsburgh. There, he prayed in front of a Baroque painting from the 1700s called "Mary Untier of

---

[247] Joseph Ratzinger, Hans Urs von Balthasar, trans. A. Walker *Mary: the Church at the Source* (San Francisco: Ignatius Press, 2005), 24.

[248] James M. Hayes, John W. Padberg, and John M. Stadenmaier, "Symbols, Devotions and Jesuits," *Studies in the Spirituality of Jesuits*, 20.3 (May 1988), 2.

Knots." The painting was commissioned by a man whose grandfather's marriage had been saved when a local Jesuit priest recommended him to pray to Mary "to untie all the knots." He did so, and peace once again reigned between him and his wife.[249] In reference to this title, the Holy Father in a Saturday papal address said:

> Mary's faith unties the knot of sin (cf. Lumen Gentium, 56). What does that mean? The Fathers of the Second Vatican Council took up a phrase of Saint Irenaeus, who states that "the knot of Eve's disobedience was untied by the obedience of Mary; what the virgin Eve bound by her unbelief, the Virgin Mary loosened by her faith" (Adversus Haereses, III, 22, 4).
>
> The "knot" of disobedience, the "knot" of unbelief. When children disobey their parents, we can say that a little "knot" is created. This happens if the child acts with an awareness of what he or she is doing, especially if there is a lie involved. At that moment, they break trust with

---

[249] Austen Ivereigh, *The Great Reformer: Francis and the Making of a Radical Pope* (New York: Henry Holt and Company, 2014), 199.

their parents. You know how frequently this happens! Then the relationship with their parents needs to be purified of this fault; the child has to ask forgiveness so that harmony and trust can be restored. Something of the same sort happens in our relationship with God. When we do not listen to him, when we do not follow his will, we do concrete things that demonstrate our lack of trust in him – for that is what sin is – and a kind of knot is created deep within us. These knots take away our peace and serenity. They are dangerous, since many knots can form a tangle which gets more and more painful and difficult to undo.

But we know one thing: nothing is impossible for God's mercy! Even the most tangled knots are loosened by his grace. And Mary, whose "yes" opened the door for God to undo the knot of the ancient disobedience, is the Mother who patiently and lovingly brings us to God, so that he can untangle the knots of our soul by his fatherly mercy. We all have some of these knots and we can ask in our heart of hearts: What are the knots in my life? "Father, my knots cannot be undone!" It is a mistake to say anything of the sort! All the knots of our heart, every knot of our conscience, can be undone. Do I ask Mary to help me trust in God's mercy, to undo those knots, to change? She, as a woman of faith, will surely tell you: "Get up, go to the Lord: he understands you". And she leads us by the hand as a Mother, our Mother, to the embrace of our Father, the Father of mercies.[250]

Discussion Questions

1. Respond to von Balthasar's description of "excesses" in Marian devotion. Do you think he is accurate? If so why? If not why not? In responding cite at least three specific examples that support your view.

2. Discuss tensions between the Liturgical Movement, and the Ecumenical Movement with the Marian movement. Include the following in your response: objective, Scripture, Revelation, subjective, patristic, and medieval.

---

[250] Pope Francis, "Prayer for the Marian Day on the Occasion of the Year of Faith: Address of Holy Father Francis," October 12, 2013, w2.vatican.va, http://w2.vatican.va/content/francesco/en/speeches/2013/october/documents/papa-francesco_20131012_preghiera-mariana.html, (accessed June 10, 2016).

3. Discuss the theological reasons why the Council Fathers decided to integrate Marian theology within *Lumen Gentium* instead of creating a separate document on Mary. Include the following in your response: Christology, Ecclesiology, isolation, ecumenical concerns, Marian and Petrine Principles.

4. Compare in specific ways the following Popes Marian Theology: Paul VI, John Paul II, Benedict XVI, and Francis. Include the following in your response: existential, personalism, hermeneutics of continuity, and devotional.

Chapter 9

Marian Dogmas

Introduction

In the following two chapters, we will study Marian dogmas and heresies that Marian dogmas counteract. We will do so in the discerning light the modern papacy provides to us. In this chapter, we will first reflect on the role of doctrine. Then, the four Marian dogmas will be presented: Perpetual Virginity, Mother of God, Immaculate Conception, and the Assumption.

251

---

251 The Yorck Project: *10.000 Meisterwerke der Malerei.* DVD-ROM, 2002, "di Cosimo Immaculate Conception, 1505," photograph, https://commons.wikimedia.org/

Role of Dogmas

According to the International Theological Commission's 1989 document *On the Interpretation of Dogmas*, "In the dogma of the Church, one is thus concerned with the correct interpretation of the Scriptures."[252] Ratzinger similarly explains, "dogma is, in fact essentially nothing other than the explanation of Scripture."[253] In another work, he adds that dogma is not to be understood "as an external shackle, but as the living source that made knowledge of the truth possible."[254] The truth, therefore, that dogma are intended to convey is the message that lies behind the words of Sacred Scripture. They are not shackles but rather keys that unlock the message behind the words of Scripture. Ultimately, this message is Christ, the Word of the Father spoken eternally in the love of the Holy Spirit.

Since dogmas have been defined throughout the history of the Church, including in recent history with the 1950 dogmatic declaration of the Assumption of Mary into heaven, some people argue that in order to renew Christianity it is necessary to go

---

wiki/File%3APiero_di_Cosimo_057.jpg, (accessed June 28, 2016).

[252] Scott Hahn, *Hail, Holy Queen* (New York: Image Books, 2001), 92.

[253] Joseph Ratzinger, *Handing on the Faith in an Age of Disbelief* (San Francisco: Ignatius Press, 2006), 17.

[254] Joseph Ratzinger, *Milestones: Memoirs 1927-1977*, trans. Erasmo Leiva-Merikakis (San Francisco: Ignatius Press, 1998), 57.

back to early Christianity in which there were fewer definitions of faith. The search for Christianity's "original essence," writes Ratzinger "is carried on today, in the era of historical consciousness, almost entirely by seeking its oldest forms and establishing them as normative. The original is confused with the primitive. By contrast the faith of the Church sees in these beginnings something living, that conforms to its own constitution only insofar as it develops."[255]

An analogy of an acorn and an oak tree can help to explain the distinction Ratzinger makes between what is original from what is primitive. Since an acorn is the origin of the oak tree, in order to understand the oak tree more fully it is important to know its origin, the acorn. However, the acorn only represents the oak tree in its primitive, unfulfilled, potential state. Similarly, knowing about the early Church is important since our current Church owes its origin to the early Church, especially since the early Church was closer in time to Jesus' incarnation than we are. We have been blessed with over two thousand years of the Holy Spirit's presence whom the Father sent into the hearts of his disciples after Jesus ascended into heaven. The Holy Spirit, working through the successors to the Apostles, has caused the Church to grow and develop analogously similar to how an

---

[255] Joseph Ratzinger, *Daughter Zion: Meditations on the Church's Marian Belief*, trans. McDermott (San Francisco: Ignatius Press, 1983), 38.

oak tree grows and develops into its fullness. One specific way the Church has developed is by clarifying doctrines, and, by so doing, providing greater access to the message behind the text of Scripture, without adding anything to the message. In light of this appreciative understanding of Church doctrines, we will now examine the four Marian dogmas.

Perpetual Virginity

The two earliest Marian dogmas that were formally taught by the Church are the Perpetual Virginity of Mary and Mary as Mother of God. We will begin with Mary's Perpetual Virginity. Reference to the "Virgin Mary" appears both in the most ancient western form and the most recent western form of the Apostolic Creed. In a c. 374 ancient exposition of the Nicene Creed, written by St. Ephipanius, bishop of Salamis in Cyprus, Mary is called "holy Mary ever-virgin."[256]

Pope St. Siricius (384-399) in his 392 epistle *Accepi litteras vestras* to the Anysiua, Bishop of Thessalonica is the first example of the Church formally teaching Mary's perpetual virginity (before, during and after giving birth to Jesus). In the epistle he writes:

Surely, we cannot deny that regard-

---

[256] Henry Denzinger, *The Sources of Catholic Dogma*, Thirtieth Edition, trans. Roy J. Deferrari (St. Louis: B. Herder Book Co., 1957), 9.

ing the sons of Mary the statement is justly censured, and your holiness has rightly abhorred it, that from the same virginal womb, from which according to the flesh Christ was born, another offspring was brought forth. For neither would the Lord Jesus have chosen to be born of a virgin, if he had judged she would be so incontinent, that with the seed of human copulation she would pollute that generative chamber of the Lord's body, that palace of the eternal King. For he who imputes this, imputes nothing other than the falsehood of the Jews, who say that he could not have been born of a virgin, For, if they accept this authority from the priests, that Mary seems to have brought forth many children, they strive to sweep away the truth of faith with greater zeal.[257]

In 534, Pope John II in his epistle *Olim quidem* to the senators of Constantinople, reaffirms Mary's perpetual virginity by defending her as an "ever

---

[257] Henry Denzinger, *The Sources of Catholic Dogma*, Thirtieth Edition, trans. Roy J. Deferrari (St. Louis: B. Herder Book Co., 1957), 39.

Virgin Mary."[258] The teaching of Mary being an "ever Virgin" is taught once again at the Council of Constantinople II (553),[259] at the Lateran Council (649)[260] and at the Third Council of Constantinople (680-681).[261] In addition, the local Council of Toledo XI (675) more explicitly affirms Mary's perpetual virginity by teaching:

> Of these three persons we believe
> that for the liberation of the human
> race only the person of the Son

[258] Henry Denzinger, *The Sources of Catholic Dogma*, Thirtieth Edition, trans. Roy J. Deferrari (St. Louis: B. Herder Book Co., 1957), 83.

[259] Henry Denzinger, *The Sources of Catholic Dogma*, Thirtieth Edition, trans. Roy J. Deferrari (St. Louis: B. Herder Book Co., 1957), 86. "Can. 3. If anyone does not confess that there are two generations of the Word of God, the one from the Father before the ages, without time and incorporeally, the other in the last days, when the same came down from heaven, and was incarnate of the holy and glorious Mother of God and ever Virgin Mary, and was born of her, let such a one be anathema."

[260] Henry Denzinger, *The Sources of Catholic Dogma*, Thirtieth Edition, trans. Roy J. Deferrari (St. Louis: B. Herder Book Co., 1957), 102. "Can. 3. If anyone does not properly and truly confess in accord with the holy Fathers, that the holy Mother of God and ever Virgin and immaculate Mary in the earliest of the ages conceived of the Holy Spirit without seed, namely, God the Word Himself specifically and truly, who was born of God the Father before all ages, and that she incorruptibly bore [Him?], her virginity remaining indestructible even after His birth, let him be condemned."

[261] Henry Denzinger, *The Sources of Catholic Dogma*, Thirtieth Edition, trans. Roy J. Deferrari (St. Louis: B. Herder Book Co., 1957), 114.

became true man without sin from the **holy and immaculate Virgin Mary**, from whom He is begotten in a new manner and by a new birth; in a new manner, because invisible in divinity, He became visible in flesh; by a new birth, however, is He begotten, because inviolate virginity without the experience of sexual intercourse supplied the material of human flesh made fruitful by the Holy Spirit. This Virgin birth is neither grasped by reason nor illustrated by example, because if grasped by reason, it is not miraculous; if illustrated by example, it will not be unique.[262]

That the virgin birth cannot be "grasped by reason," since there is no other example of the virgin birth in history, signifies, as Ratzinger demonstrates, that God with Mary began anew by creating a new sinless creation, "the necessary

---

[262] Henry Denzinger, *The Sources of Catholic Dogma*, Thirtieth Edition, trans. Roy J. Deferrari (St. Louis: B. Herder Book Co., 1957), 109-110. The paragraph continues with, "Yet we must not believe that the Holy Spirit is Father of the Son, because of the fact that Mary conceived by the overshadowing of the same Holy Spirit, lest we seem to assert that there are two Fathers of the Son, ... we do not say that the Virgin Mary gave birth to the unity of the Trinity, but only to the Son, who alone assumed our nature in the unity of His person."

origin"[263] for the birth of Jesus.[264] In response to the objection that the Church's teaching on the virgin birth is a late tradition, Ratzinger argues, "The literary form may be relatively late, but the tradition given in that form had already existed in another form; no historical critique can exclude the possibility that the simple nucleus of the account is significantly more ancient."[265] In other words, the late public official reception of the teaching on virgin birth does not necessarily mean that the tradition itself is late.

According to another objection to the virgin birth of Jesus, this belief was derived from ancient mythology: Egyptian Mythology, the Greek Virgin Goddess Diana, the Roman cult of the Great Mother etc. In response to this objection, Ratzinger argues, "There are only motifs which touch on the Christian assertion more or less closely. I see nothing negative in this: these may be the expression of a psychological archetype in whose

---

[263] Joseph Ratzinger, *Daughter Zion: Meditations on the Church's Marian Belief*, trans. McDermott (San Francisco: Ignatius Press, 1983), 51.

[264] Joseph Ratzinger, *Daughter Zion: Meditations on the Church's Marian Belief*, trans. McDermott (San Francisco: Ignatius Press, 1983), 47-48.

Joseph Ratzinger, *Daughter Zion: Meditations on the Church's Marian Belief*, trans. McDermott (San Francisco: Ignatius Press, 1983), 54. He continues with, "Furthermore, the agreement with regard to the nucleus of the account from two mutually independent traditions which otherwise show considerable formal diversities in detail is a norm of some significance—and this is what we can ascertain through a study of the sources of Matthew and Luke."

confused longing, as in all authentic archetypes, a deep knowledge of reality is expressed. Be the reality ever so remote, the human heart with its intimations and anticipatory questions already awaits its fulfillment."[266]

When the historical objections to the virgin birth are examined carefully, it is revealed, further argues Ratzinger, that the conviction of the objectors cannot come from history. Rather, it is located in a particular world view. Ratzinger defines a world view as "a synthesis of knowledge and values, which together propose to us a total vision of the real, a vision whose evidence and power of persuasion rest upon the fusion of knowledge and value."[267] Since values are often subjective and not based on historical data, determining the truth of a claim on the basis of a world view is necessarily problematic.

In the case of those who are convinced that the virgin birth is impossible, value is confused with knowledge. Conviction that a virgin birth is impos-

---

[266] Joseph Ratzinger, *Daughter Zion: Meditations on the Church's Marian Belief*, trans. McDermott (San Francisco: Ignatius Press, 1983), 56. In his essay, *Myth Became Fact*, C.S. Lewis similarly defends Christianity from those who resorting to the fallacy "post hoc, ergo propter hoc" argue that Christianity is derived from myths. C.S. Lewis, *God in the Dock* (Grand Rapids: Wm. B. Eerdmans Publishing Co., 1970), 54-60.

[267] Joseph Ratzinger, *Daughter Zion: Meditations on the Church's Marian Belief*, trans. McDermott (San Francisco: Ignatius Press, 1983), 57.

sible is based on an evaluation stemming from one's world view and not from knowledge alone. This becomes clear when we look to knowledge that can be obtained by the scientific method. The modern scientific method cannot disprove the possibility of a virgin birth occurring. It can only indicate that a virgin birth is highly improbable. This is because the scientific method deals with probabilities and not with certainties.[268] In addition, just because it is highly improbable for an event to occur does not mean that it is impossible for God to intervene in nature to bring about the event. According to the worldview influenced by the Catholic faith, what is improbable in the world is possible by God since He created the world, sustains the world in existence, and, when He chooses, intervenes in the world.[269] The Marian doctrine of the virgin birth supports these three ways of God's creative activity.[270]

---

[268] Joseph Ratzinger, *Daughter Zion: Meditations on the Church's Marian Belief*, trans. McDermott (San Francisco: Ignatius Press, 1983), 57-59.

[269] Joseph Ratzinger, *Daughter Zion: Meditations on the Church's Marian Belief*, trans. McDermott (San Francisco: Ignatius Press, 1983), 60.

[270] Von Balthasar's biblical defense of the virgin birth complements Ratzinger's more logical defense. Von Balthasar writes, "It is Zechariah who, after having been struck dumb on account of his unbelief, is asked what name his son shall be given and finally sings the Benedictus: "And his father Zechariah was filled with the Holy Spirit, and prophesied, saying, 'Blessed be the Lord God of Israel'" (Lk 1:67–68). After these preliminaries, we would expect to learn a great deal about Joseph, the man descended from David on whom the whole

We will conclude this section on the virgin birth by briefly responding to a common Protestant objection that since the New Testament refers to brothers of Jesus (Mark 6:3, Matthew 13:55-56, Galatians 1:19, 1 Corinthians 9:5) at some point Mary lost her virginity. To answer this objection,

---

promise depends. But the entire scene of the Annunciation, both in Matthew and in Luke, passes over him and concentrates entirely on Mary. Here for the first time the angel of the Lord addresses a woman, and it is she who transmits the Spirit whom she has received to another woman, her cousin Elizabeth, who only then is filled with the Holy Spirit and receives the sign of the child leaping in her womb. Mary alone sings the Magnificat. It is quite clear that something much more than 'biological generation' is going on here, namely, the decisive appearance of God as the sole Father, an appearance that excludes a relation to another father to the same degree that Jesus' spousal relation to his bride, the Church, rules out any other marital relation for him. Abraham's loins had been blessed by the Holy Spirit, who reawakened their life-giving powers. The old servant Eliezer had to touch them in order to seal his oath to provide Isaac with a bride. Surely Joseph's life-giving powers would have received much more praise if they had finally brought forth the long-awaited scion of David. But no. The whole process of bodily begetting, in fact, the whole question of whether a man or woman is fruitful or not, loses its importance in the New Covenant. Joseph crosses the threshold of the New Covenant by an act of renunciation. In this way he becomes the foster father of the one who himself will be a virgin and through a most radical renunciation will open a completely different source of life. His crucified body as a whole will be endowed with power to beget and, according to Paul, will produce his immaculate bride without spot or wrinkle, the Church." Joseph Ratzinger, Hans Urs von Balthasar, trans. A. Walker *Mary: the Church at the Source* (San Francisco: Ignatius Press, 2005), 151-152.

the term brother, as it was used in Scripture, needs to be defined. In explaining how the term brother was understood at the time of Jesus by Jesus and his people, Scott Hahn states:

> The Hebrew word for 'brother' is a more inclusive term, applying to cousins as well. In fact, in ancient Hebrew there is no word for cousin. To a Jew of Jesus' time, one's cousin was one's brother. This familial principle applied in other Semitic languages as well, such as Aramaic, the language Jesus spoke. Furthermore, precisely because Jesus was an only child, His cousins would even assume the legal status of siblings for Him, as they were His nearest relatives. Finally, the word "firstborn" raises no real difficulty, because it was a legal term in ancient Israel that applied to the child who "opened the womb," whether or not the mother bore more children afterward.[271]

The broad, inclusive definition of the term brother at the time of Jesus and before is evident in the Old Testament (Genesis 13:8, 14:12) and in the New Testament. For example, although James and

---

[271] Scott Hahn, *Hail, Holy Queen* (New York: Image Books, 2001), 104. Cf. Genesis 13:8, 14:12,

Joseph are called brothers of Jesus (Mark 6:3), they later are identified in Scripture as the sons of another Mary. (Matthew 27:56, Mark 15:40).[272]

Another objection is in reference to Matthew chapter one, verse twenty-five. "When Joseph woke from sleep, he did as the angel of the Lord commanded him; he took his wife, but knew her not until she had borne a son; and he called his name Jesus." (NRSV) According to the objectors of the virgin birth, the "until" of this verse indicates that after Mary bore a son, Joseph "knew" her by having sexual relations with her. In response to this common objection, Matthew Leonard explains that the use of "until" does not mean that a change occurred after Jesus was born. For example, when I say, "May the Lord bless you until we meet again," the "until" is not commonly interpreted as indicating that I want God to stop blessing the person after we meet in the future. The same logic can be applied to Jesus' words to his apostles when he said, "I am with you always, even unto the end of the world."[273] Most Christians will agree that Jesus did not intend with the word "until" to indicate that when we see him at the end of the world he will stop being with

---

[272] Matt Fradd, "Jesus had Brothers?" September 17, 2013, catholic.com, http://www.catholic.com/blog/matt-fradd/jesus-had-brothers, (accessed June 12, 2016).

[273] Tim Staples, *Behold Your Mother: A Biblical and Historical Defense of the Marian Doctrines* (El Cajon: Catholic Answers, 2014), 186.

us.[274]

Mother of God

The third ecumenical Council of Ephesus (431) condemned the teaching of Nestorius, Patriarch of Constantinople (386-450 AD), while defending the teaching that Mary is the Mother of God. Nestorius erroneously taught that Mary only gave birth to Christ but not to God (*Theotokos*). He made this assertion since although he distinguished between Jesus' human and divine natures he failed to unite the two natures (sources of action) in the one divine person (the who of action)[275] of Jesus Christ:

1. If anyone does not confess that Emmanuel is God in truth, and therefore that the holy virgin is the mother of God. (for she bore in a fleshly way the Word of God become flesh), let him be anathema.

2. If anyone does not confess that the Word from God the Father has been united by hypostasis with the flesh and is one Christ with his own flesh, and is therefore God and man together, let him be anathema.[276]

In 451, the Council of Chalcedon further clari-

---

[274] Matthew Leonard, *The Bible and the Virgin Mary Journey Through Scripture*, Participant Workbook (Steubenville: St. Paul Center for Biblical Theology, 2014), 69.

[275] Called *hypostasis* in tradition.

[276] Norman P. Tanner, *Decrees of the Ecumenical Councils*, Volume I (District of Columbia: Georgetown University Press, 1990), 59.

fied the relationship of Christ's two natures by stating that, "the property of both natures is preserved and comes together into a single person and a single subsistent being; he is not parted or divided into two persons, but is one and the same only-begotten Son, God, Word, Lord Jesus Christ...."[277] Since Christ's human and divine natures are united in the one divine person of Jesus Christ, what is experienced by one nature of Christ was experienced by the person of Christ. For this reason, one may say that Jesus, the Son of God, truly was born of Mary and truly died on the cross (in his human nature not in his divine nature). The theological principle that describes this application of a nature of Christ to the divine person of Christ is called the communication of idioms. Mary, therefore, did not give birth only to Jesus' human nature, but as the opener of the Council of Ephesus Saint Cyril of Alexandria explains[278] gave birth to a person and not only to a nature.[279]

Tim Staples, with reference to Fr. Pacwa, similarly defends Mary as Mother of God by pointing out the false logic of the following Protestant argument.

---

[277] Norman P. Tanner, *Decrees of the Ecumenical Councils*, Volume I (District of Columbia: Georgetown University Press, 1990), 86.

[278] Norman P. Tanner, *Decrees of the Ecumenical Councils*, Volume I (District of Columbia: Georgetown University Press, 1990), 37.

[279] Scott Hahn, *Hail, Holy Queen* (New York: Image Books, 2001), 100.

Major premise: Jesus is God
Minor premise: Mary is the Mother of Jesus
Conclusion: Mary is the Mother of God

Major premise: God is Trinity
Minor premise: Mary is the Mother of God
Conclusion: Mary is the Mother of the Trinity[280]

The fallacy that is made in the second syllogism is called the fallacy of the undistributed middle term. The second syllogism's middle term is God. This term needs to be distributed properly according to how the term ought to be defined. In the second syllogism, the term God is not distributed properly because it is being defined by God as Trinity. However, the term God in the first syllogism, which the middle term of the second syllogism is defined by, only refers to the second person of the Blessed Trinity who is God but is not the Trinity.[281]

Mary's privileged status of physically being the Mother of God distinguishes her motherhood from the spiritual motherhood to which all believers of Jesus are called. By our baptism, we are called to

---

[280] Tim Staples, *Behold Your Mother: A Biblical and Historical Defense of the Marian Doctrines* (El Cajon: Catholic Answers, 2014), 28.

[281] Tim Staples, *Behold Your Mother: A Biblical and Historical Defense of the Marian Doctrines* (El Cajon: Catholic Answers, 2014), 28.

spiritually conceive of Christ and allow him to grow within us. Due to Mary's being both Mother of God physically and spiritually, her participation in Christ's one mediation distinguishes her mediative role from ours, while, at the same time, always subordinate to Christ's mediation.[282]

Immaculate Conception

In 1854, Pope Pius IX in his apostolic constitution *Ineffabilis Deus* solemnly defined the Marian doctrine of the Immaculate Conception. He wrote:

> We declare, pronounce, and define that the doctrine which holds that the most Blessed Virgin Mary, in the first instance of her conception, by a singular grace and privilege granted by Almighty God, in view of the merits of Jesus Christ, the Savior of the human race, was preserved free from all stain of original sin, is a doctrine revealed by God and therefore to be believed firmly and constantly by all the faithful.[283]

---

[282] Antoine Nachef, *Mary's Pope: John Paul II, Mary, and the Church Since Vatican II* (Franklin: Sheed & Ward, 2000), 148.

[283] Pius IX, "Ineffabilis Deus," December 8, 1854, ewtn.com,

As was shown in the chapter on the medieval age, Mary's being immaculately conceived was not accepted by all theologians, including prominent ones such as St. Thomas Aquinas. After the above teaching was defined, "if," Pope Pius IX strongly asserts:

> anyone shall dare--which God forbid!--to think otherwise than as has been defined by us, let him know and understand that he is condemned by his own judgment; that he has suffered shipwreck in the faith; that he has separated from the unity of the Church; and that, furthermore, by his own action he incurs the penalties established by law if he should dare to express in words or writing or by any other outward means the errors he think in his heart.[284]

In his definition of the Immaculate Conception, Pius IX carefully teaches that Mary was redeemed by Jesus Christ in an anticipatory man-

https://www.ewtn.com/faith/teachings/marye1.htm, (accessed June 12, 2016).

[284] Pius IX, "Ineffabilis Deus," December 8, 1854, ewtn.com,
https://www.ewtn.com/faith/teachings/marye1.htm, (accessed June 12, 2016).

ner by being preserved from sin. God could do this since by eternally existing outside of time He can apply the fruits of His son's redemption before His son's incarnation and after his son's crucifixion.[285] In 1483, in his Constitution *Grave nimis*, Pope Sixtus IV, (1471-1484) similarly taught:

> We reprove and condemn assertions of this kind as false and erroneous and far removed from the truth, and also by apostolic authority and the tenor of these present [letters] we condemn and disapprove on this point published books which contain it . . . [but these also we reprehend] who have dared to assert that those holding the contrary opinion, namely, that the glorious Virgin Mary was conceived with original sin are guilty of the crime of heresy and of mortal sin, since up to this time there has been no decision made by the Roman Church and the Apostolic See.[286]

How do we explain some Fathers of the Church

---

[285] Matthew Leonard, *The Bible and the Virgin Mary Journey Through Scripture*, Participant Workbook (Steubenville: St. Paul Center for Biblical Theology, 2014), 108.

[286] Henry Denzinger, *The Sources of Catholic Dogma*, Thirtieth Edition, trans. Roy J. Deferrari (St. Louis: B. Herder Book Co., 1957), 237.

and Saints erred on matters of faith, such as the Immaculate Conception, that had not yet been defined in their time? Blessed John Henry Newman (1801-1909) answers this by explaining that although no one can add to public revelation,

> as time goes on, what was given once for all is understood more and more clearly. The great Fathers and Saints in this sense have been in error, that, since the matter of which they spoke had not been sifted and the Church had not spoken, they did not in their *expressions do justice to their own real meaning...* Now, as to the doctrine of the Immaculate Conception, it was *implied* in early times, and never *denied*. In the Middle Ages it was denied by St. Thomas and by St. Bernard, but they took the phrase in a different sense from that in which the Church now takes it. They understood it with reference to our Lady's mother, and thought it contradicted the text, "In sin hath my mother conceived me"— whereas *we* do not speak of the Immaculate Conception except as relating to Mary; and the other doctrine (which St. Thomas and St. Bernard did oppose) *is* really

heretical.[287]

The passage from Scripture that Newman quotes is from Psalm 51. This verse is similar to a verse found in Romans "the righteousness of God through faith in Jesus Christ for all who believe. For there is no distinction, since all have sinned and fall short of the glory of God." (Romans 3:22-23 NRSV). The verse from the New Testament seems to indicate more than Psalm 51 does, which is in the singular, that all human beings without exception have sinned. Matthew Leonard shows how this is interpretation is false by demonstrating that the passage needs to be read in its proper context in order to be interpreted properly. In the just quoted verse from Romans, Paul is comparing two groups, Jewish and non-Jewish, in relationship to sin. With respect to sin, both groups, without "distinction" have sinned. He does not mean, though, that every individual within these two groups have not sinned since he also teaches that Jesus is sinless.[288] It was

---

[287] John Henry Newman, "Memorandum on the Immaculate Conception, newmanreader.org, http://www.newmanreader.org/works/meditations/meditatio ns3.html#note1, (accessed June 12, 2016). "This Memorandum is given as written off by the Cardinal for Mr. R. I. Wilberforce, formerly Archdeacon Wilberforce, to aid him in meeting the objections urged by some Protestant friends against the doctrine of the Immaculate Conception. The *italics* are the Cardinal's."

[288] Matthew Leonard, *The Bible and the Virgin Mary Journey Through Scripture*, 5 DVDs (Steubenville: St. Paul Center for Biblical Theology, 2014); Matthew Leonard, *The*

most fitting for the sinless Jesus to be born of a sinless woman.

The following analogy from Leonard helps to shed light on why it was most fitting for Mary to be Immaculately conceived.[289] As a priest purifies a vessel that will hold the precious blood of Jesus, so too did God purify, in an anticipatory manner, the vessel which was to bear His son for nine months, Mary's womb.[290]

Assumption

In 1950, Venerable Pope Pius XII, heeding the growing number of "postulations and petititions"[291] solemnly defined Mary's Assumption into heaven in his apostolic constitution *Munificentissimus Deus*. Notice that the papal definition does not indicate as to whether Mary died before she was assumed into heaven. Whether Mary died or did not die before her assumption is a theological issue which theologians may currently and legitimately debate, as

Bible and the Virgin Mary Journey Through Scripture, Participant Workbook (Steubenville: St. Paul Center for Biblical Theology, 2014), 108.

[289] "Our tainted nature's solitary boast" as William Wordsworth (1770-1850) wrote in his poem, *The Virgin*.

[290] Matthew Leonard, *The Bible and the Virgin Mary Journey Through Scripture*, 5 DVDs (Steubenville: St. Paul Center for Biblical Theology, 2014).

[291] Pius XII, "Munificentissimus Deus," November 1, 1950, no. 8, w2.vatican.va, http://w2.vatican.va/content/pius-xii/en/apost_constitutions/documents/hf_p-xii_apc_19501101_munificentissimus-deus.html, (accessed June 13, 2016).

long as they do so in a way that does not bring scandal.[292]

> 44. ... [B]y the authority of our Lord Jesus Christ, of the Blessed Apostles Peter and Paul, and by our own authority, we pronounce, declare, and define it to be a divinely revealed dogma: that the Imma-culate Mother of God, the ever Virgin Mary, having completed the course of her earthly life, was assumed body and soul into heavenly glory.
>
> ...
>
> 47. It is forbidden to any man to change this, our declaration, pronouncement, and definition or, by rash attempt, to oppose and counter it. If any man should presume to make such an attempt, let him know that he will incur the wrath of Almighty God and of the Blessed Apostles Peter and Paul.[293]

---

[292] Matthew Leonard, *The Bible and the Virgin Mary Journey Through Scripture*, Participant Workbook (Steubenville: St. Paul Center for Biblical Theology, 2014), 125.

[293] Pius XII, "Munificentissimus Deus," November 1, 1950, no. 44, 47, w2.vatican.va, http://w2.vatican.va/content/pius-xii/en/apost_constitutions/documents/hf_p-xii_apc_19501101_munificentissimus-deus.html, (accessed June 13, 2016).

One of the earliest references to Mary's Assumption is found in the fourth century text, *Passing of the Blessed Virgin Mary*. The highly detailed, extravagant nature of this text may cause some to dismiss it. However, even if the details are exaggerated and fanciful, the text does bear witness to an early belief in Mary's bodily assumption into heaven.[294]

> 16. Then the Savior said: Let it be according to your opinion. And He ordered the archangel Michael to bring the soul of St. Mary. And, behold, the archangel Michael rolled back the stone from the door of the tomb; and the Lord said: Arise, my beloved and my nearest *relation;* thou who hast not put on corruption by intercourse with man, suffer not destruction of the body in the sepulchre. And immediately Mary rose from the tomb, and blessed the Lord, and falling forward at the feet of the Lord, adored Him, saying: I cannot render sufficient thanks to Thee, O Lord, for Thy boundless benefits which Thou hast deigned to bestow upon me Thine handmaiden. May Thy name, O Redeemer of the world, God of Israel, be blessed

---

[294] Scott Hahn, *Hail, Holy Queen* (New York: Image Books, 2001), 109.

forever.

17. And kissing her, the Lord went back, and delivered her soul to the angels, that they should carry it into paradise. And He said to the apostles: Come up to me. And when they had come up He kissed them, and said: Peace be to you! as I have always been with you, so will I be even to the end of the world. And immediately, when the Lord had said this, He was lifted up on a cloud, and taken back into heaven, and the angels along with Him, carrying the blessed Mary into the paradise of God. And the apostles being taken up in the clouds, returned each into the place allotted for his preaching, telling the great things of God, and praising our Lord Jesus Christ, who liveth and reigneth with the Father and the Holy Spirit, in perfect unity, and in one substance of Godhead, for ever and ever. Amen.[295]

---

[295] "The Passing of the Blessed Virgin Mary," no. 16-17, ccel.org, http://www.ccel.org/ccel/schaff/anf08.vii.xliv.html, (accessed June 13, 2016).From *Anti-Nicene Fathers, Volume 8, The Twelve Patriarchs, Excerpts and Epistles, The Clementia, Apocrypha, Decretals, Memoirs of Edessa and Syriac Documents, Remains of the First.*

Two more reliable sources for Mary's Assumption are the writings of Saint Gregory of Tours (c. 538-594) and Saint John of Damascus (c. 675-749), also known as Saint John Damascene.[296]

~ St. Gregory of Tours on the Assumption ~

At daybreak, however, the Apostles took up her [Mary's] body on a bier and placed it in a tomb; and they guarded it, expecting the Lord to come. And behold, again the Lord stood by them; and the holy body having been received, He commanded that it be taken in a cloud into paradise: where now, rejoined to the soul, [Mary] rejoices with the Lord's chosen ones, and is in the enjoyment of the good of an eternity that will never end.[297]

~ St. John of Damascus on the Assumption ~

Today the spotless Virgin, untouched by earthly affections, and all

---

[296] "St. John Damascene on Holy Images Followed by Three Sermons on the Assumption, trans. Mary H. Allies," gutenberg.org, http://www.gutenberg.org/files/49917/49917-h/49917-h.html, (accessed June 13, 2016).

[297] Rod Bennet, *Four Witnesses: The Early Church in Her Own Words* (San Francisco: Ignatius Press, 2002), 335. The following source is cited. Gregory of Tours, *Eight Books of Miracles* 1, 4, in FEF 3:306, no. 3388a.

heavenly in her thoughts, was not dissolved in earth, but truly entering heaven, dwells in the heavenly tabernacles. Who would be wrong to call her heaven, unless indeed he truly said that she is greater than heaven in surpassing dignity? ... [H]ow could she, who brought life to all, be under the dominion of death? ... [H]ow shall she, who received the Life Himself, without beginning or end, or finite vicissitudes, not live forever. ... How could corruption touch the life-giving body? These are things quite foreign to the soul and body of God's Mother. Death trembled before her. In approaching her Son, death had learnt experience from His sufferings, and had grown wiser. The gloomy descent to hell was not for her, but a joyous, easy, and sweet passage to heaven. If, as Christ, the Life and the Truth says: 'Wherever I am, there is also my minister,' how much more shall not His mother be with Him? She brought Him forth without pain, and her death, also, was painless.[298]

---

[298] "Sermon II On the Assumption in St. John Damascene on Holy Images Followed by Three Sermons on the Assumption, trans. Mary H. Allies," no. gutenberg.org,

A common objection to the doctrine of the Assumption is that since the earliest writings which refer to Mary's assumption date at the earliest to the fourth century, this doctrine is insufficiently witnessed to by history. In countering this objecttion, Matthew Leonard points out that while there may be no historical records earlier than the fourth century on Mary's Assumption, there also are no historical records during the first century of the Christian era that reject belief in Mary's Assumption. It is reasonable to conclude, therefore, that the absence of such a denial indicates Mary's Assumption was universally believed in a similar way that Christ's Resurrection was believed by early Christians.

Also, Leonard further argues, there are no writings from early Christianity in which someone claims to have relics of Mary, or knows where her bones are, or knows where her reliquary or gravesite is. Historical witnesses from this time, however, testify to churches and cities competing with one another for bones of holy men and women. At times the competition for relics from holy men and women was very intense. It is reasonable to conclude, therefore, that if Christians knew where the bones of Mary were, then the competition for her relics would have been the most intense of all saints. An explanation of why such a competition never was recorded is because since

http://www.gutenberg.org/files/49917/49917-h/49917-h.html, (accessed June 13, 2016).

Mary was Assumed into heaven no competition for her relics took place. In place of written accounts indicating where her body was buried, where her bones were enshrined and the subsequent competition for her bones, there are two cities that are referred to in ancient writings as the sites of Mary's empty tomb: Jerusalem and Ephesus.[299]

---

[299] Matthew Leonard, *The Bible and the Virgin Mary Journey Through Scripture*, 5 DVDs (Steubenville: St. Paul Center for Biblical Theology, 2014). Ratzinger has a slightly different take from Leonard's historical interpretation of the doctrine of the Assumption. Joseph Ratzinger, *Daughter Zion: Meditations on the Church's Marian Belief*, trans. McDermott (San Francisco: Ignatius Press, 1983), 72-73. "So it is clear that the point at issue [Mary's Assumption] cannot be historical tradition of an historical fact; the affirmation is misunderstood if it is considered or presented as such. This makes it decisively different from Jesus' resurrection. Doubtless his resurrection also transcends history and in this sense offers us no historical fact of the usual type, but it is essential for the resurrection that it reach into temporal existence and announce itself in an historical account. The text of the Bull of 1950 did justice to this distinction insofar as it does not speak of Mary's *resurrectio* (*anastasis*), but of her *assumptio ad coelestem gloriam*—not of "resurrection", but of the "assumption" of the body and soul into heavenly glory. In this way it clearly defines the content of the article of faith as a theological, not an historical, affirmation. ...Here we face the even more insistent objection that the raising of Mary is a fact that must be witnessed and communicated, not just invented. This was behind the emphatic protest of German theology before the official proclamation of the dogma, most insistently in the famous series of articles by B. Altaner, whose entire historical erudition demonstrated that, as far as sources are concerned, there is no witness to such a doctrine before the sixth century. So it is clear that the point at issue cannot be historical

Discussion Questions

1. From a Catholic perspective, discuss the role of dogmas in the Church. Include the following in your response: message/meaning of Scripture, primitive, original, development, Holy Spirit, and an analogy other than the acorn and oak tree analogy presented in the chapter.

2. Respond to the objections on Mary's Perpetual Virginity. Include the following in your response: late public reception, tradition, derived from ancient mythology, world view, the scientific method and probability, God's creative power, brothers

---

tradition of an historical fact; the affirmation is misunderstood if it is considered or presented as such. This makes it decisively different from Jesus' resurrection. What then does this mean? To clarify the matter, one would have to pay attention to the dogma's historical development and the factors in its formulation. This would show that the decisive driving force behind the declaration was veneration for Mary, that the dogma, so to speak, owes its origin, impetus, and goal more to an act of homage than to its content. This also becomes clear in the text of the dogmatic proclamation, where it is said that the dogma was promulgated for the honor of the Son, for the glorification of the mother, and for the joy of the entire Church. This dogma was intended to be an act of veneration, the highest form of Marian praise. What the orient achieves in the form of liturgy, hymns, and rites, took place in the occident through the form of a dogmatic proclamation, which was intended to be, so to speak, a most solemn form of hymnology. This is how it should be understood. It distinguishes the last two Marian dogmas in a certain respect from the earlier form of ecclesial confessions, even though the doxological element always played a more or less accentuated role."

of Jesus or the "until" in Matthew chapter one, verse twenty-five.

3. Respond to objections on Mary as Mother of God. Include the following in your response: communication of idioms, God in reference to Jesus, and God in reference to the Trinity.

4. Respond to objections on the Immaculate Conception. Include the following in your response: God is outside of time, the Redemption of Christ, development of doctrine and theological errors of Saints, Romans chapter two, verses twenty-two and twenty-three.

5. Respond to objections on the Assumption. Include the following in your response: Pope Pius XII unilaterally taught this doctrine, insufficiently witnessed to by history, relics of holy men and women in early Christianity, and Mary's empty tomb.

Chapter 10

Marian Doctrine and Heresies

Introduction

According to Saint Louis de Montfort (1673-1716), whose writings had a profound influence on John Paul II,[300] "Mary ... says the Church (and the Holy Ghost, who guides the Church), who alone makes all heresies come to naught."[301] Montfort's

---

[300] In the introductory section to Montfort's *True Devotion* book a quote from John Paul II is given, "The reading of this book was a decisive turning-point in my life. I say 'turning-point,' but in fact it was a long inner journey . . . This 'perfect devotion' is indispensable to anyone who means to give himself without reserve to Christ and to the work of redemption." . . ." It is from Montfort that I have taken my motto: 'Totus tuus' (' I am all thine'). Someday I'll have to tell you Montfortians how I discovered De Montfort's Treatise on True Devotion to Mary, and how often I had to reread it to understand it." Louis de Montfort, *True Devotion to Mary: With Preparation for Total Consecration*, trans. Frederick William Faber (Kindle Edition: Catholic Way Publishing, 2013), 2.

[301] Louis de Montfort, *True Devotion to Mary: With Preparation for Total Consecration*, trans. Frederick William Faber (Kindle Edition: Catholic Way Publishing, 2013), 108. Montfort continues with, "we may be sure that, however critics may grumble, no faithful client of Mary will ever fall into heresy or illusion, at least formal. He may very well err

presentation of Mary and true Marian devotion as a destroyer of heresies is rooted in tradition. Representing this tradition, Pius IX described Mary as she "who has destroyed all heresies and snatched the faithful people and nations from all kinds of direst calamities".[302]

Similarly, Pius XI in his encyclical on the rosary, *Ingravescentibus Malis* (1937) states, "When, in fact, errors everywhere diffused were bent upon rending the seamless robe of the Church and upon throwing the Catholic world into confusion, our fathers turned with confident soul to her 'alone who destroys all heresies in the world' (Roman Breviary), and the victory won through her brought the return of tranquility."[303] Similarly, but less directly, *Lumen Gentium* describes Mary as she who "unites in her person and re-echoes the greatest teachings [doctrines] of the Faith."[304]

---

materially, take falsehood for truth, and the evil spirit for the good; and yet he will do even this with more difficulty than others. But sooner or later he will acknowledge his material fault and error; and when he knows it, he will not be in any way self-opinionated in believing and maintaining what he had once thought true."

[302] Pius IX, "*Ineffabilis Deus*: Apostolic Constitution," Dec. 8, 1854, papalencyclicals.net, http://www.papalencyclicals.net/Pius09/p9ineff.htm, (accessed June 14, 2016).

[303] Pius XI, "*Ingravescentibus Malis*: Encyclical of Pope Pius XI on the Rosary," 1937, no. 2, w2.vatican.va, http://w2.vatican.va/content/pius-xi/en/encyclicals/documents/hf_p-xi_enc_29091937_ingravescentibus-malis.html, (accessed June 14, 2016).

[304] "*Lumen Gentium*," 1964, no. 65, Vatican.va, http://www.vatican.va/archive/hist_councils/ii_vatican_coun

In this chapter, we will see how adherence to Marian doctrine helps one to remain faithful to the truths of the Catholic faith, to the truth of Jesus Christ. In so doing, the following heresies in relationship to Marian teachings will be discussed: Nestorians, Theo-monism, Pelagianism, Fideism, Rationalism, and Gnosticism.

305

cil/documents/vat-ii_const_19641121_lumen-gentium_en.html, (accessed June 14, 2016).

305   http://www.ofs-mariaimmacolata.it/immacolata/immacolata.htm, "Antonio Ciseri, immacolata. Firenze, Chiesa

Nestorianism

In the preceding chapter, Nestorianism was touched upon in relationship to the Mary as Mother of God. In 431, the Council of Ephesus condemned the heresy of Nestorianism named after Nestorius, the Patriarch of Constantinople. Nestorius' heresy was teaching that Mary is only the Mother of Jesus's human nature alone and, therefore, cannot be called Mother of God. This is not correct, since women, including Mary, give birth to persons not to only natures. In the case of Mary, she gave birth to the person of Jesus Christ in which his divine and human natures are united. The later Council of Chalcedon (451) further clarified the union of Jesus' two natures by teaching that:

> [W]e all with one voice teach the confession of one-and the same Son, our Lord Jesus Christ: the same perfect in divinity and perfect in humanity, the same truly God and truly man, of a rational soul and a body; consubstantial with the Father as regards his divinity, and the same consubstantial with us as regards his humanity; like us in all respects except for sin; begotten before the ages from the Father as

del Sacro Cuore," photograph, https://commons.wikimedia .org/wiki/File%3AAntonio_Ciseri%2C_immacolata._Firenze% 2C_Chiesa_del_Sacro_Cuore.jpg (accessed June 28, 2016).

regards his divinity, and in the last days the same for us and for our salvation from Mary, the virgin God-bearer, as regards his humanity; one and the same Christ, Son, Lord, only-begotten, acknowledged in two natures which undergo no confusion, no change, no division, no separation; at no point was the difference between the natures taken away through the union, but rather the property of both natures is preserved and comes together into a single person and a single subsistent being; he is not parted or divided into two persons, but is one and the same only-begotten Son, God, Word, Lord Jesus Christ...[306]

In condemning Nestorianism, the Council Fathers at Chalcedon also condemned the opposite heresy of Nestorianism formulated by Eutyches. Nestorius was right in maintaining a distinction between the two nature of Jesus. He fell into heresy, however, by refusing to acknowledge that these two natures are united without confusion or mixture in the divine person of Jesus Christ. Due to the hypostatic union, what Jesus experienced in

---

[306] Norman P. Tanner, *Decrees of the Ecumenical Councils*, Volume I (Washington, DC: Georgetown University Press, 1990), 86.

one nature may be attributed to the divine person. This means that since Mary gave birth to Jesus's bodily, human nature, she, at the same time, gave birth to the divine person in who Jesus' human nature is united to Jesus' divine nature. The opposite heresy, which Eutyches in over reacting to Nestorius taught, "introduce[ed] a confusion and mixture, and mindlessly imagin[ed] that there is a single nature of the flesh and the divinity."[307]

Ratzinger has an interesting take on the importance of the Council of Ephesus's and the Council of Chalcedon's condemnation of Nestorius's insistence that Mary only gave birth to Christ's human nature and not to the person of Christ. He writes, "behind the formula 'Mother of God' stands the conviction that the unity of Christ is so profound that the merely corporeal Christ can nowhere be distilled out of it, because in man the corporeal is also the human-corporeal, as modern biology confirms."[308] Nestorius's division of Jesus into two distinct, unrelated, separate natures reveals an underlying problematic understanding of who a human being is, who God is, and how God has redeemed man.

With respect to man, if one understands the biological element as totally divorced from the

---

[307] Norman P. Tanner, *Decrees of the Ecumenical Councils*, Volume I (Washington, DC: Georgetown University Press, 1990), 84.

[308] Joseph Ratzinger, *Daughter Zion: Meditations on the Church's Marian Belief*, trans. McDermott (San Francisco: Ignatius Press, 1983), 34.

personal-human element within a human being then the following logical conclusions can be made. It does not make a difference what my body does, as long as I as a human person make a good intention. Also, being a man or woman is determined by an individual personal choice. With respect to God, Nestorius's strict separation within Jesus can lead one to conclude that the incarnation did not affect all of human nature since the divine never really was united nor really was related to Jesus's human nature. Because of this strict separation, the rest of human nature was not affected by Christ, since even Christ's human nature was not related to his divine nature. On the practical level, this can then cause one to question the practice of "offering up our sufferings," since it is erroneously assumed that the suffering cannot be really united to Christ's divinity in order for the sufferings to be transformed and redeemed.

Theo-monism and Pelagianism

As defined by von Balthasar, the heresy of theo-monism is the belief that human beings can only relate to the divine in a passive manner with no activity on the part of the human. In order to flesh out this abstract definition of theo-monism we can turn to the medieval philosopher from India, Shankara (788-822 AD). Shankara wrote an influential commentary on a foundational text of Indian philosophy and religion called the Vedas, which is considered by Hindus as their most sacred text. The part of the Vedas on which Shankara wrote are the highly spiritual and philosophical sections called the Upanishads (c. 900-500 BC).[309] The fundamental principle of Shankara's philosophy may be summarized as "Atman is Brahman."[310] Brahman, for Shankara, is the universal, underlying divine energy that relates all individual things to one another. Atman refers to the individual things themselves. According to Shankara's four principles, since "Atman is Brahman" or the individual is the divinity, difference between what is divine and what is not is merely fictional.[311] The way to become divine, therefore, is to passively let go of one's individuality in order to be completely absorbed into the divine.

The opposite heresy of theo-monism's extreme passivism is Pelagianism which errs by excessively stressing action to the detriment of reception. The founder of Pelagianism, Pelagius, (c. 300s-400s) taught that human beings do not need grace in order to be virtuous and be saved.[312] We have it in

---

[309] Grant Hardy, *Great Minds of the Eastern Intellectual Tradition*, Lectures 1-18 (Chantilly: The Teaching Company, 2011), 18; Online Etymology Dictionary, http://etymonline.com/, (accessed June 12, 2015).

[310] Jeanneane D. Fowler, *Perspectives of Reality: An Introduction to the Philosophy of Hinduism* (Brighton: Sussex Academic Press, 2002), 239.

[311]W. J. Johnson, *Oxford Dictionary of Hinduism* (New York: Oxford University Press, 2009), 37, 64.

[312] Brinley Roderick Rees, *Pelagius: Life and Letters* (Woodbridge: The Boydell Press, 1991), 15-25. Rees

our own natural powers, he argued, to sufficiently imitate Christ. As well argued by St. Augustine, the Doctor of Grace, in order to imitate Christ as St. Paul encourages with, "Be imitators of me, as I am of Christ," (1 Cor. 11:1 NRSV) we need the help of grace. St. Paul teaches this in Ephesians, "For by grace you have been saved through faith, and this is not your own doing; it is the gift of God— not the result of works, so that no one may boast." (Eph. 2: 8-9) Teaching in accordance with St. Paul, Augustine writes, "For God has not only given us the ability and aids it, but He further works in us 'to will and to do.' It is not because we do not will, or do not do, that we will and do nothing good, but because we are without His help."[313]

Notice in these verses, written by Augustine against Pelagian teaching, Augustine both affirms man's need to act while maintaining that we cannot act properly without receiving the grace of God. In locating the Catholic orthodox position that, like Augustine's, rejects both Pelagianism and theo-monism, von Balthasar maintains that an orthodox theology of salvation stands between theo-monism and Pelagianism. Von Balthasar names the ortho-dox position theo-dramatic where God and human

---

demonstrates that when Pelagius views are examined it becomes less evident to what extent he held heretical views.

[313] Augustine, "A Treatise on the Grace of Christ, and on Original Sin," in *Saint Augustin: Anti-Pelagian Writings*, Vol. 5 (New York: Christian Literature Company, 1887), 227.

beings act together in the drama of salvation.[314] With reference to theatre, von Balthasar explains how God relates to us. He describes salvation history as a drama with the author of the drama as God the Father, the Holy Spirit as the Director of the drama and Jesus as the lead actor of the drama.[315]

Through Mary, the gospel's Annunciation scenes represent the orthodox position defended above. Mary is receptive, but with her Fiat, with her yes to God, she is receptive in an active way, not only at the Annunciation but throughout her life. Both Mary as creature and the grace of God is affirmed at the Annunciation as cooperating together, with of course grace always being primary.[316]

---

[314] Brendan Leahy, *The Marian Profile* (New York: New City Press, 2000), 51. With reference to theatre, von Balthasar describes salvation history as a drama with God the Father as the author, the Holy Spirit as the Director, and Jesus as the lead actor of the drama. In order to interpret von Balthasar's use of terminology from theatre properly it is important to remember he is using these terms analogously. One essential difference between acting in the drama of salvation and acting on a stage is that the former is shaped by a mission given to us by God. We are, consequently, to identify with our missions so that we become the role He has assigned to us.

[315] An orthodox theology of salvation stands between theomonism (human beings are only passive recipients of salvation) and Pelagianism. Brendan Leahy, *The Marian Profile* (New York: New City Press, 2000), 51.

[316] Joseph Ratzinger, *Daughter Zion: Meditations on the Church's Marian Belief*, trans. McDermott (San Francisco: Ignatius Press, 1983), 28, 32-33. "To deny or reject the feminine aspect in belief, or, more concretely, the Marian

Fideism and Rationalism

The gospel's description of Mary at the Annunciation not only reveals to us the orthodox understanding of the relationship between grace and human nature, between God and his creation, which is neither theo-monism nor Pelagian, but also reveals the proper understanding of the relationship of reason to faith. The error of those who excessively emphasize reason to the detriment of faith by attributing to reason what only faith can give is rationalism. The error of those who excessively emphasize faith to the detriment of reason by attributing to faith what reason can know apart from faith is fideism.[317]

---

aspect, leads finally to the negation of creation and the invalidation of grace. It leads to a picture of God's omnipotence that reduces the creature to a mere masquerade and that also completely fails to understand the God of the Bible, who is characterized as being the creator and the God of the covenant—the God for whom the beloved's punishment and rejection themselves become the passion of love, the cross. ...in modern times, either inducing a rebellion against Mariology or driving it into a dangerous romanticism. Wherever the unity of Old and New Testaments disintegrates, the place of a healthy Mariology is lost. Likewise, this unity of the Testaments guarantees the integrity of the doctrines of creation and of grace. In modern times, however, the loss of typological exegesis (seeing the cohesion of the one history in the many histories) has actually led to the separation of the Testaments, and by isolating the doctrine of grace it has at the same time increasingly threatened the doctrine of creation."

[317] Pope John Paul II, "Fides et Ratio," no. 52, w2.vatican.va, http://w2.vatican.va/content/john-paul-

As well presented by John Paul II in his writings on Mary, the gospel accounts of Mary reveal a woman who only "in faith and through faith" believes in the truth of her son. Mary's example also, John Paul II points out, teaches us that reason has an important role to play in our journey of faith. Her question to the Angel Gabriel at the Annunciation and her question to her son in the Temple (Lk. 2:48-50) indicate that God wants us to be conscious and intellectually aware of his mysterious designs that unfold in the course of time.[318] In number seventeen of *Redemptoris Mater,* the Holy Father presents Mary from the perspective of faith seeking understanding:

When the Holy Family returns to

---

ii/en/encyclicals/documents/hf_jp-ii_enc_14091998_fides-et-ratio.html, (accessed May 16, 2016). In his encyclical letter, Fides et Ratio, John Paul II condemns fideism and rationalism by asserting, "If the Magisterium has spoken out more frequently since the middle of the last century, it is because in that period not a few Catholics felt it their duty to counter various streams of modern thought with a philosophy of their own. At this point, the Magisterium of the Church was obliged to be vigilant lest these philosophies developed in ways which were themselves erroneous and negative. The censures were delivered even-handedly: on the one hand, fideism and radical traditionalism, for their distrust of reason's natural capacities, and, on the other, rationalism and ontologism because they attributed to natural reason a knowledge which only the light of faith could confer."

[318] Antoine Nachef, *Mary's Pope: John Paul II, Mary, and the Church Since Vatican II* (Franklin: Sheed & Ward, 2000), 132-134.

Nazareth after Herod's death, there begins the long period of the hidden life. She "who believed that there would be a fulfillment of what was spoken to her from the Lord" (Lk. 1:45) lives the reality of these words day by day. And daily at her side is the Son to whom "she gave the name Jesus"; therefore in contact with him she certainly uses this name, a fact which would have surprised no one, since the name had long been in use in Israel. Nevertheless, Mary knows that he who bears the name Jesus has been called by the angel "the Son of the Most High" (cf. Lk. 1:32). Mary knows she has conceived and given birth to him "without having a husband," by the power of the Holy Spirit, by the power of the Most High who overshadowed her (cf. Lk. 1:35), just as at the time of Moses and the Patriarchs the cloud covered the presence of God (cf. Ex. 24:16; 40:34-35; I Kings 8:10-12). Therefore, Mary knows that the Son to whom she gave birth in a virginal manner is precisely that "Holy One," the Son of God, of whom the angel spoke to her.

During the years of Jesus' hidden life in the house at Nazareth, Mary's life too is "hid with Christ in God" (cf. Col. 3:3) through faith. For faith is contact with the mystery of God. Every day Mary is in constant contact with the ineffable mystery of God made man, a mystery that surpasses everything revealed in the Old Covenant. From the moment of the Annunciation, the mind of the Virgin-Mother has been initiated into the radical "newness" of God's self-revelation and has been made aware of the mystery. She is the first of those "little ones" of whom Jesus will say one day: "Father, ...you have hidden these things from the wise and understanding and revealed them to babes" (Mt. 11:25). For "no one knows the Son except the Father" (Mt. 11:27). If this is the case, how can Mary "know the Son"? Of course she does not know him as the Father does; and yet she is the first of those to whom the Father "has chosen to reveal him" (cf. Mt. 11:26-27; 1 Cor. 2:11). If though, from the moment of the Annunciation, the Son-whom only the Father knows completely, as the one who begets him in the eternal "today" (cf. Ps. 2:7) was revealed to Mary, she, his Mother, is in contact with the truth about her Son only in faith and through faith! She is therefore blessed, because "she has believed," and continues to believe day after day amidst all the trials and the adversities of Jesus' infancy and then during the years of the hidden life at Nazareth, where he "was obedient to them" (Lk. 2:51). He was obedient both to Mary and also to Joseph, since Joseph took the place of his father in people's eyes; for this reason, the Son of Mary was regarded by the people as "the carpenter's son" (Mt. 13:55).

The Mother of that Son, therefore, mindful of what has been told her at the Annunciation and in subsequent events, bears within herself the radical "newness" of faith: the beginning of the New Covenant. This is the beginning of the Gospel, the joyful Good News. However, it is not difficult to see in that beginning a particular heaviness of heart, linked with a sort of night of faith"-to use the words of St. John of the Cross-a kind of "veil" through which one has

to draw near to the Invisible One
and to live in intimacy with the
mystery. And this is the way that
Mary, for many years, lived in
intimacy with the mystery of her
Son, and went forward in her
"pilgrimage of faith," while Jesus
"increased in wisdom...and in favor
with God and man" (Lk. 2:52). God's
predilection for him was manifested
ever more clearly to people's eyes.
The first human creature thus
permitted to discover Christ was
Mary, who lived with Joseph in the
same house at Nazareth.

However, when he had been found
in the Temple, and his Mother asked
him, "Son, why have you treated us
so?" the twelve-year-old Jesus
answered: "Did you not know that I
must be in my Father's house?" And
the Evangelist adds: "And they
(Joseph and Mary) did not understand the saying which he spoke to
them" (Lk. 2:48-50). Jesus was
aware that "no one knows the Son
except the Father" (cf. Mt. 11:27);
thus even his Mother, to whom had
been revealed most completely the
mystery of his divine sonship, lived
in intimacy with this mystery only

through faith! Living side by side with her Son under the same roof, and faithfully persevering "in her union with her Son," she "advanced in her pilgrimage of faith," as the Council emphasizes. And so it was during Christ's public life too (cf. Mk. 3:21-35) that day by day there was fulfilled in her the blessing uttered by Elizabeth at the Visitation: "Blessed is she who believed."[319]

Gnosticism

John Paul II's affirmation that Mary freely, consciously, and personally with her intellect and will continually gave her consent to God not only, explains Leahy, is a rejection of rationalism and fideism but also is a rejection of Gnosticism.[320]

---

[319] John Paul II, "*Redemptoris Mater*," no. 17, w2.vatican.va, http://w2.vatican.va/content/john-paul-ii/en/encyclicals/documents/hf_jp-ii_enc_25031987_redemptoris-mater.html, (accessed June 15, 2016).

[320] John Paul II, "*Veritatis Splendor*," no. 120, w2.vatican.va, http://w2.vatican.va/content/john-paul-ii/en/encyclicals/documents/hf_jp-ii_enc_06081993_veritatis-splendor.html, (accessed June 15, 2016). "Mary lived and exercised her freedom precisely by giving herself to God and accepting God's gift within herself. Until the time of his birth, she sheltered in her womb the Son of God who became man; she raised him and enabled him to

Gnosticism (from a Greek word *gnosis* meaning knowledge) erroneously believes that knowledge and not faith and grace is sufficient for a person to experience salvation. People who have pronounced gnostic tendencies tend to excessively spiritualize doctrinal truths to such an extent that the historical nature of these truths is ignored and understood as secondary or even completely irrelevant.[321]

For example, one example of a modern gnostic understanding of Christ's resurrection is that it is unimportant whether Christ rose from the dead. Instead, what is important is that Christians are to allow the narrative of Christ's resurrection from the dead to inform their political practices by forming communities who with "resurrection" hope fight for a new world where justice will reign.

With a simple diagram in a conversation with Marisa Cerini, von Balthasar showed how proper Marian devotion and belief help to prevent a Catholic from falling into the above-mentioned heresies. In recounting the conversation, Marisia said:

---

grow, and she accompanied him in that supreme act of freedom which is the complete sacrifice of his own life. By the gift of herself, Mary entered fully into the plan of God who gives himself to the world. By accepting and pondering in her heart events which she did not always understand (cf. Lk 2:19), she became the model of all those who hear the word of God and keep it (cf. Lk 11:28), and merited the title of "Seat of Wisdom"."

[321] Antoine Nachef, *Mary's Pope: John Paul II, Mary, and the Church Since Vatican II* (Franklin: Sheed & Ward, 2000), 57, 166.

As I see it – he said – just like Mary and her ecclesial dimension, the four members each represent a fundamental dimension of the Church: Peter represents "ministry," John "love," Paul "novelty" and "freedom in the Spirit," James, bishop of Jerusalem after Peter's departure, "tradition" and "fidelity to the tradition." At that point he drew a shape on the chalkboard distributing each of these in four different points in the shape of a cross – Peter to the right, John to the left, James above and Paul below. He then traced an ellipse around them by way of indicating Mary who embraces everyone.[322]

As explained by von Balthasar, Mary, as Mother of God and Mother of the Church, holds all the dimensions of the Church together. She embraces the Petrine dimension of hierarchy and structure. She embraces Pauline dimension of missionary innovation and creativity. She embraces the Jacobine dimension, represented by James, the Lesser, who represents continuity with tradition.

---

[322] Brendan Leahy, *The Marian Profile* (New York: New City Press, 2000), 138. In reference to Marisa Cerini, "Dimensione mariana" in Unita e Carismi 8(1998)/1, 2-4.

(Remember James the Lesser was the one who helped to reconcile the different views at the Jerusalem council. He argued that Gentiles not be required to be circumcised or refrain from eating pork but be required to refrain from eating meat from strangled animals. (Acts 15:13-31)) Finally, Mary embraces the Johannine dimension of contemplation of the heavenly world to come. Leahy in commenting on these four-fold dimensions that von Balthasar refers to states:

> If any one of the four major principles should be separated or made absolute, the Marian profile [representing Catholic orthodoxy] of the Church would suffer.

> If, for instance the Jacobine element of law and tradition is one-sidedly emphasized, we end up with positivism and integralism, a reactionary clinging to obsolete forms.

> Should the Petrine-institutional dimension loom large, the Church's visage becomes distorted in organization and administration.

> If the Pauline characteristic of freedom in the Spirit is unilaterally highlighted, the result is rationalism and dogmaticism, a diplomatic up-

dating following what is popular and fashionable.

Finally, an excess on the part of the Johannine principle flows into Gnosticism, pneumatism and love as "experience," mere universal humanitarian kindness focusing on change in social structures.[323]

Discussion Questions

1. Discuss how Mary, as *Lumen Gentium* states, "re-echoes the greatest teachings of the Faith." Do so in four specific ways.

2. How did the Council of Ephesus and the Council of Chalcedon reject Nestorianism? Include the following in your response: Nestorius, Eutyches, person, nature, and underlying theological and anthropological principles of Nestorius's teachings.

3. Discuss how Mary's role in Scripture, as interpreted by Catholic doctrine, reveals the errors of both theo-monism and Pelagianism. Include the following in your response: theo-monism, Pelagianism, activity, passivity, grace, and the Annunciation.

---

[323] Brendan Leahy, *The Marian Profile* (New York: New City Press, 2000), 138-139.

4. Discuss how Mary's role in Scripture, as interpreted by Catholic doctrine, reveals the errors of both Fideism and Rationalism. Include the following in your response: Fideism, Rationalism, Annunciation, faith, knowledge, and awareness.

5. Discuss how Mary's role in Scripture, as interpreted by Catholic doctrine, and Mary's role in the Church is contrary to Gnosticism. Include the following in your response: Gnosticism, doctrine, history, spiritualization, dimensions of the Church.

Chapter 11

Mary and Ecclesiology

Introduction

The last chapter ended with von Balthasar showing how Mary encompasses all the dimensions of the Church. Von Balthasar describes Mary in this manner because she is both Mother of God, as Mother of Christ, and Mother of Church, by being Mother of the mystical body whose head is Christ. As Mother of the Church, Mary is closely identified with the Church. If we, therefore, want to know the Church better, it is necessary to know Mary for as a saying goes, "No Mary, No Jesus. Know Mary, Know Jesus,"[324] where Jesus refers both to the second person of the blessed Trinity and to Christ's mystical body of the Church. In accordance with the logic, this chapter will reflect on the mystery of the Church from a Marian perspective. We will do so with respect to the identification of Mary with the Church, Mary as Church archetype, Mary and the Church as heaven,

---

[324] Tim Staples, *Behold Your Mother: A Biblical and Historical Defense of the Marian Doctrines* (El Cajon: Catholic Answers, 2014), 10.

and Ecclesial and Marian Mediation.

325

Identification of Mary and the Church

The German theologian Matthias Joseph Scheeben (1835-1888) was particularly noted for his Mariology. Scheeben described Mary's relationship with the Church as a mutual indwelling.[326] Within this mutual indwelling, Scheeben calls a *perichoresis*, Mary and the Church are identified while remaining distinct. The complementary distinction between the two can be clarified from the perspective of objectivity and subjectivity. In Mary's subjective faith the objective truth of Divine Revel-

---

[325] Art Renewal Center, "A Western depiction of the Pentecost, painted by Jean II Restout, 1732.," photograph, https://commons.wikimedia.org/wiki/File%3AJean_II_Restout_-_Pentec%C3%B4te.jpg, (accessed June 28, 20167).

[326] Brendan Leahy, *The Marian Profile* (New York: New City Press, 2000), 23.

ation, given to us through the Church, is perfectly realized. Members of the Church, regardless of their role, are to emulate Mary by striving not only to adhere intellectually to the objective truth of Divine Revelation, which, due to our human condition, comes to us through the medium of propositions, but also to allow Divine Revelation to so influence us that we become more and more like Christ who is truth in person.

The objective and subjective dimensions of the Church are interrelated with another relationship named by von Balthasar as external functions and inner spirit. According to von Balthasar, "If one divides the living bond between the external and internal (or objective and subjection, the institutional and existential) spirits and defines the forms of states of life in the Church purely sociologically, then one has already abandoned the place where Church is *mysterium*."[327] When the external

---

[327] Hans Urs von Balthasar, *Explorations in Theology, Vol. 4: Spirit and* 163. Later in the same volume von Balthasar relates both the objective and subjective dimensions of the Church to the Holy Spirit. "As a general rule we can say that the Holy Spirit always lives in the Church as objective as well as subjective Spirit: as institution or rule, or *disciplina*, and as inspiration and loving obedience to the Father in this spirit of adoption. Neither one can be separated from the other, since we stand under the law of Christ who should assume form in us, and not just as the servant of God exerting himself with his labors on earth but also as the Risen One ascended into heaven (Eph 2:6), so that our 'life with Christ is hidden in god'. Certainly 'if Christ our life appears, you will also appear with him in glory' (Col 3:3-4). And then the institutional aspect of

dimension of the Church is emphasized to the exclusion of the internal spirit the result can be doing the right deed for the wrong reason which is "the greatest treason" as T.S. Elliot reminds us in *Murder in the Cathedral* through Thomas Becket's fourth tempter.[328] De Lubac described this temptation as "the most subversive temptation" for on the outside all seems to be well but is not since the "spiritual perfections" and good acts that are being done are for man's glory and not for God's.[329]

---

the Church will disappear in the same way as it did for the risen Lord and take on the aspect of adoption as God's children. For then we will no longer need to learn obedience but will have it be instinct and as part of our freedom, and the Spirit will tower over us objectively only in his divine original meaning – as witness and igniter of love." Hans Urs von Balthasar, *Explorations in Theology, Vol. 4: Spirit and* 239.

[328] T.S. Eliot, *Murder in the Cathedral* (Orlando: Harcourt Brace & Company, 1963), 44. "The last temptation is the greatest treason. To do the right deed for the wrong reason."

[329] Henri de Lubac, *The Splendor of the Church*, trans. Michael Mason (San Francisco: Ignatius Press, 1999), Location 4075-4081 of 8029. "That is Mary; and so also is the Church our Mother-the perfect worshipper; there lies the focal point of the analogy between them, for there the same spirit is at work in both. But whereas this humble and lofty perfection shines dazzlingly in supreme purity in Mary, in ourselves (who are as yet barely touched by the Spirit) it scarcely struggles to the light at all. The Church-as-Mother is never at the end of her labor to deliver us to the life of the Spirit, and the greatest danger we are to the Church, the most subversive temptation, the one that is ever and insidiously reborn when all the rest are overcome, and even strengthened by those victories, is what Abbot Vonier called the temptation to 'worldliness of the mind... the practical relinquishing of other-worldliness, so that moral and even spiritual standards should be based, not on the

In reference to these words of De Lubac, the future pope Cardinal Bergoglio responded to the question, "what is the worst thing that can happen in the Church?" with "It is what De Lubac calls 'spiritual worldliness'. It is the greatest danger for the Church, for us, who are in the Church. 'It is worse,' says De Lubac, 'more disastrous than the infamous leprosy that disfigured the dearly beloved Bride at the time of the libertine popes.' Spiritual worldliness is putting oneself at the center. It is what Jesus saw going on among the Pharisees: 'You glorify yourselves. Who give glory to yourselves, the ones to the others.'"[330]

---

glory of the Lord, but on what is the profit of man; an entirely anthropocentric outlook would be exactly what we mean by worldliness. Even if men were filled with every spiritual perfection, but if such perfections were not referred to God (suppose this hypothesis to be possible) it would be unredeemed worldliness. If this spiritual worldliness were to invade the Church and set to work to corrupt her by attacking her very principle, it would be something infinitely more disastrous than any worldliness of the purely moral order-even worse than the hideous leprosy that at certain moments in history inflects so cruel a disfigurement on the Bride; when religious seems to set up the scandalous 'in the sanctuary itself...."

[330] Sefania Falasca, "What I would have said at the Consistory: An Interview with Cardinal Jorge Mario Bergoglio, Archbishop of Buenos Aires," *30Days*, Issue no. 11 (2007), 30giorni.it, http://www.30giorni.it/articoli_id_16457_l3.htm, (accessed June 16, 2016).

Mary as Church Archetype

In summarizing the patristic era Marian teaching, von Balthasar states, "They realize that Mary is the type of the Church, not as a mere 'foreshadowing' (as the types of the Old Testament foreshadow the truth of the New Covenant), but as an archetype, that is, as the perfectly, unsurpassably realized 'Idea' of the Church.[331] Ratzinger described Mary in a similar way with respect to Mary's Immaculate Conception. Mary's Immaculate Conception he ex-plains, "reflects ultimately faith's certitude that there really is a holy Church—as a person and in a person."[332]

Not only is Mary in her origin, in her birth, the archetype, the Church in her perfection, but also in her definitive state in heaven. Mary, Ratzinger later adds, "stands for the Church itself, for its definitive state of salvation, which is no longer a promise awaiting fulfillment but a fact."[333] The opening prayer of the mass for the Feast of the Immaculate Conception brings forth the relationship of the sinless Mary as the ideal in person that the Church, referred to as "us," is to strive to become in order to

---

[331] Joseph Ratzinger, Hans Urs von Balthasar, trans. A. Walker *Mary: the Church at the Source* (San Francisco: Ignatius Press, 2005), 141.

[332] Joseph Ratzinger, *Daughter Zion: Meditations on the Church's Marian Belief*, (San Francisco: Ignatius Press, 1983), 70.

[333] Joseph Ratzinger, *Daughter Zion: Meditations on the Church's Marian Belief*, (San Francisco: Ignatius Press, 1983), 79.

experience the salvation of Christ:

> Let us pray, [That through the prayers of the sinless Virgin Mary, God will free us from our sins.] Father, You prepared the Virgin Mary to be the worthy mother of your son. You let her share beforehand in the salvation Christ would bring by his death, and kept her sinless from the first moment of her conception. Help us by her prayers to live in your presence without sin. We ask this through our Lord Jesus Christ, your Son, who lives and reigns with you and the Holy Spirit, one God, for ever and ever.[334]

Notice in this prayer the doctrinal truth of Mary's Immaculate Conception is directed toward the greater truth and fullness of truth who is Jesus Christ.[335] All doctrinal truths of Mary are directed toward her Son Jesus since, borrowing the words of John Paul II, in the Incarnation Christ and Mary are "indissolubly joined." In this union with Christ

---

[334] "Immaculate Conception Prayers," churchyear.net, http://www.churchyear.net/icprayers.html, (accessed Mary 12, 2016).

[335] Matthew Leonard, *The Bible and the Virgin Mary Journey Through Scripture*, 5 DVDs (Steubenville: St. Paul Center for Biblical Theology, 2014).

as "Lord and Head," Mary "prefigures the Church's condition as spouse and mother."[336]

Mary and the Church as Heaven

In order to understand the relationship of Mary and the Church to heaven, heaven needs to be defined. In describing heaven, St. Pope John Paul II in a General Audience said, "'heaven ... is neither an abstraction nor a physical place in the clouds, but a living, personal relationship with the Holy Trinity."[337] The Church Father St. John Damascus (675-749) spoke about heaven in a similar personal manner by identifying heaven with Mary. According to him, Mary is the new heaven. In one of his sermons he said, "This heaven [Mary] is

---

[336] John Paul II, "Redemptoris Mater," no. 1, w2.vatican.va, http://w2.vatican.va/content/john-paul-ii/en/encyclicals/documents/hf_jp-ii_enc_25031987_redemptoris-mater.html, (accessed May 15, 2016).

[337] John Paul II, "Heaven is Fullness of Communion with God, Papal General Audience, July 21, 1999," ewtn.com, http://www.ewtn.com/library/PAPALDOC/JP2HEAVN.HTM, (accessed June 16, 2016). The entire quote is "In the context of Revelation, we know that the 'heaven or 'happiness' in which we will find ourselves is neither an abstraction nor a physical place in the clouds, but a living, personal relationship with the Holy Trinity. It is our meeting with the Father which takes place in the risen Christ through the communion of the Holy Spirit. It is always necessary to maintain a certain restraint in describing these "ultimate realities" since their depiction is always unsatisfactory. Today, personalist language is better suited to describing the state of happiness and peace we will enjoy in our definitive communion with God."

clearly much more divine and awesome than the first. Indeed he who created the sun in the first heaven would himself be born of this second heaven, as the Sun of Justice."[338] In explaining how Mary encompasses and surpasses heaven as the new heaven St. John Damascus preached:

> O how did heaven receive her who is greater than heaven? How did she, who had received God, descend into the grave? This truly happened, and she was held by the tomb. It was not after bodily wise that she surpassed heaven. For how can a body measuring three cubits, and continually losing flesh, be compared with the dimensions of heaven? It was rather by grace that she surpassed all height and depth, for that which is divine is incomparable.[339]

---

[338] Luigi Gambero, *Mary and the Fathers of the Church: The Blessed Virgin Mary in Patristic Thought*, trans. Thomas Buffer (San Francisco: Ignatius Press, 1991), 402. The following was referenced. John Damascene, *Homily on the Nativity*, 3: PG 96, 664 D.

[339] St. John Damascene, "Sermon I: On the Assumption in St. John of Damascene on Holy Images (Followed by Three Sermons on the Assumption)" p. 168-169, ccel.org, http://www.ccel.org/ccel/damascus/icons.html (accessed June 16, 2016).

The Church on earth provides us with a fore-taste of the heavenly Marian dimension of heaven where we will be definitively united to Christ. This principally occurs through the sacramental life of the Church. With reference to an Eastern Catholic mystic, Cardinal Schönborn describes how the sacraments reveal heaven to us:

> [P]ast and present are not the only dimensions of the sacraments; the sacraments also point to the future. To use an image of the Byzantine lay mystic Saint Nicolaus Cabasilas..., the sacraments are the "gates of heaven" through which Christ comes to meet us. In his beautiful and profound book on the three sacraments of initiation-baptism, confirmation, and the Eucharist-this spiritual master of the fourteenth century describes how the sacraments in a certain way lead us into the future, how in them heaven already opens up to us. Saint Paul speaks of the Holy Spirit as the "first fruits" of the glory to come. We can apply those words to the sacraments: they are a 'foretaste' of heaven (CCC 1130).[340]

---

[340] Christoph Schonborn, *Living the Catechism of the Catholic Church: Volume Two The Sacraments*, trans. John Saward (San Francisco: Ignatius Press, 2000), 27. He

Mary's Maternal and Ecclesial Sacramental Mediation

The Church, principally through the sacraments, and Mary, as mother, collaborate in the redemption with Christ as the One Mediator.[341] John Paul II locates Mary's maternal mediation as taking place in an intensive manner at the foot of the cross. "After her Son's departure" instructs the John Paul II, "her motherhood remains in the Church as maternal mediation."[342] At the foot of the cross, Mary's motherhood was transformed into maternal mediation, explains John Paul II:

> [I]n this pilgrimage to the foot of the Cross...Mary's motherhood itself underwent a singular transformation, becoming ever more imbued with "burning charity" towards all those to whom Christ's mission was directed. Through this "burning charity," which sought to achieve, in

references the following source. Nicolaus Cabasilas, *The Life in Christ* (Crestwood, N.Y.: St. Vladimir's Seminary Press), 1974.

[341] "For there is one God; there is also one mediator between God and humankind, Christ Jesus, himself human, who gave himself a ransom for all." (1 Timothy 2:5 NRSV)

[342] John Paul II, "Redemptoris Mater," no. 40, w2.vatican.va, http://w2.vatican.va/content/john-paul-ii/en/encyclicals/documents/hf_jp-ii_enc_25031987_redemptoris-mater.html, (accessed June 17, 2016).

union with Christ, the restoration of "supernatural life to souls," Mary entered, in a way all her own, into the one mediation "between God and men" which is the mediation of the man Christ Jesus. If she was the first to experience within herself the supernatural consequences of this one mediation-in the Annunciation she had been greeted as "full of grace" - then we must say that through this fullness of grace and supernatural life she was especially predisposed to cooperation with Christ, the one Mediator of human salvation. And such cooperation is precisely this mediation sub-ordinated to the mediation of Christ.[343]

Discussion Questions

1. Discuss how Mary is identified with the Church. Include in your response the following: *perichoresis*, objective, subjecttive, external, internal, and spiritual worldliness. (Please read the corresponding footnotes prior to responding.)

---

[343] John Paul II, "Redemptoris Mater," no. 39, w2.vatican.va, http://w2.vatican.va/content/john-paul-ii/en/encyclicals/documents/hf_jp-ii_enc_25031987_redemptoris-mater.html, (accessed June 17, 2016).

2. Discuss how Mary is the archetype of the Church. Include in your response the following: foreshadowing, Immaculate Conception, Assumption into Heaven, and the hierarchy of truth.

3. Discuss Mary and the Church in relationship to heaven. Include the following in your response: personal definition of heaven, sacraments, new heaven.

4. In relationship to Christ as the one mediator, discuss the subordinate mediating role of Mary and the Church. Include the following in your response: one mediator, subordinate mediation, sacraments, maternal mediation, "burning charity" quote from John Paul II.

Chapter 12

Marian Apparitions and Modern Day Applications of Marian Teachings

Introduction

This final chapter will introduce the two earliest Marian apparitions along with nine major Church sanctioned Marian apparitions. These apparitions personalized doctrine, in particular Marian doctrine, and greatly helped many to apply the truth of revelation to their lives. We will conclude this chapter with a reflection on how the Marian dimension of the Church aids people to grow in holiness by becoming ever more in communion with Christ and His Church, and thereby growing in love of God and neighbor.

Marian Apparitions

This section will begin with a New Testament Marian apparition, and will be followed by the earliest reference in the patristic era to a Marian apparition. Then, the following chronological selection of approved Marian apparitions will be discussed: Our Lady of Guadalupe, Our Lady of Laus,

344

344 Anonymous, "Page from *Ilustração Portuguesa*, 29 October 1917, showing the people looking at the Sun during the Fátima apparitions attributed to the Virgin Mary," photograph, https://commons.wikimedia.org/wiki/File%3ANewspaper_fatima.jpg, (accessed June 28, 2016).

Our Lady of the Miraculous Medal, Our Lady of La Salette, Our Lady of Lourdes, Our Lady of Pontmain, Our Lady of Knock, Our Lady of Fatima, Our Lady of Beauraing, Our Lady of Banneux, Our Lady of Akita, Our Lady of Kibeho, and Our Lady of Betania.

The numerous, public apparitions of Mary, who is described in Scripture as humble, meek and in the background, may surprise some. Von Balthasar's words on Marian apparitions helps to explain this apparent contradiction:

> Something analogous happens in other apparitions. Is it not almost shocking to see the lowly, humble handmaid step forward in this way in our times and even to point to herself? Is this compatible with our image of her?
>
> There are two things we can say. Mary's humility is not that of the contrite sinner; rather, it is a blithe, unselfconscious, childlike humility that would never get the idea that anything she had was her property instead of God's gift. "All generations will call me blessed": these words already show the distinctive quality of her humility. When she steps forward, it is to point through

herself to God's grace, very much in the way that Christ says, "My teaching is not mine, but his who sent me" (Jn 7:16), and "He who has seen me has seen the Father" (Jn 14:9).[345]

Revelation 12 to John the Apostle

Matthew Leonard suggests that the woman in Revelation chapter twelve may be considered as the first, recorded Marian apparition.[346] In this passage, a woman "clothed with the sun, with the moon under her feet, and on her head a crown of twelve stars" appears to the author of Revelation, identified in chapter one as John. (Revelation 12:1 NAB) The author also refers to himself as John in the following chapters and verses: 1:1, 4, 9; 22:8). Even though he does not state that he is the Apostle John, early Church Fathers referred to this John as the Apostle John. These Church Fathers include Justin Martyr, Irenaeus, Clement of Alexandria, Hippolytus, and Athanasius.[347]

---

[345] Joseph Ratzinger, Hans Urs von Balthasar, *Mary: the Church at the Source,* trans. A. Walker (San Francisco: Ignatius Press, 2005), 123.

[346] Matthew Leonard, *The Bible and the Virgin Mary Journey Through Scripture*, 5 DVDs and Participant Workbook (Steubenville: St. Paul Center for Biblical Theology, 2014).

[347] Peter S. Williamson, *Revelation: Catholic Commentary on Sacred Scripture* (Grand Rapids: Baker Publishing Co.,

Gregory Thaumaturgus (the Wonder-Worker)

St. Gregory Thaumaturgus (213-270) was born in Cappadocian Pontus to pagan parents. From 233 to 238, he was taught by Origin, who at the same time taught a number of other students. Around the time Gregory was being instructed by Origin, he embraced the Catholic faith and was baptized. Due to Gregory's fine mind and leadership ability, Phaidimos, bishop of the metropolis of Cappadocian Pontus, had Gregory ordained a bishop.[348] Gregory was not only known for his intellectual and leadership abilities, but he was also known for his mysticism. Gregory of Nyssa's *Life of Gregory Thaumaturgus* describes some of the mystical experiences of Gregory. This account contains what is reputed to be the first patristic era recorded account of a Marian apparition:

> As he [Gregory Thaumaturgus] laid awake, there appeared to him in a vision an aged person in human form adorned with solemn raiment and whose countenance was striking by great virtue and kindness in addition to the integrity his form.

2015), 19. Williamson also includes the early Christian writers Tertullian, and Origen.

[348] Gregory Thaumaturgus, *St. Gregory Thaumaturgus: Life and Works*, trans. Michael Slusser (Washington: Catholic University of America Press, 1998), 1-2

[Gregory] was struck by fear at this sight and rising up from bed, realized who he was and why he came. After quieting his fear, he said in a soft voice that a divine order bade him to appear, the reasons of which were obscure to [Gregory], in order to reveal the truth of correct belief and to encourage him to speak while gazing upon him with both joy and respect. Then the old man suddenly extended his hand and with his finger pointed to something which appeared near him which was a splendid female form instead of a male one. Once again [Gregory] was terrified and turned his face away, unable to bear its sight. The vision was especially amazing since the night was gloomy, for it resembled something like a light illuminated by another light. Since he could not look upon this spectacle, he heard from those who appeared to him speaking in detail about what he was seeking. Not only was he revered with regard to true knowledge of faith but recognized the names of each man who appeared when they called each other by their respective names. It is claimed that this vision of a female form told [Gregory] that the evangelist John was exhorted to manifest the mystery of truth to a young man, saying that she was chosen to be the mother of the Lord whom she cherished. He also said that this fitting vision had vanished again from his sight. He was immediately ordered to write down this divine revelation and later proclaim it in the church. In this way it became for others a divinely given legacy through which the people might repulse any evil of heresy. The words of that revelation are as follows:

One God, Father of the living Word (who consists of wisdom, power and who is the eternal pattern), perfect Begetter of who is perfect, Father of the Only Begotten Son. One Lord alone from him who is alone, God from God, pattern and image of the divinity, mighty Word, wisdom which encompasses everything, true Son of true Father, unseen [Son] of the unseen [Father], immortal [Son] of the immortal [Father], and eternal [Son] of the eternal [Father]. One Holy Spirit whose life is from God and who was made manifest through the Son (as well as to men), perfect image of the perfect Son, living source of those who are alive, holy provider of sanctity in whom God the Father appeared who is above all and in all, and God the Son who is in all. Perfect Trinity to whom belongs glory, eternity and kingship which can never change.[349]

Our Lady of Guadalupe

It is believed that in 1531 Mary appeared four times to St. Juan Diego on a hill called Tepeyac near the Aztec village of Tlatelolco. The first time Mary appeared to Juan Diego she told him:

You must know and be very certain in your heart, my son, that I am truly the perpetual and perfect Virgin Mary, holy Mother of the True God through whom everything lives, the Creator and Master of Heaven and Earth. I wish and intensely desire that in this place my sanctuary be erected so that in it I may show and make known and give all my love, my compassion, my help, and my protection to the people. I am your

---

[349] Gregory of Nyssa, "The Life of Gregory the Wonderworker," Documenta Catholica Omnia, http://documentacatholicaomnia.eu (accessed June 18, 2016).

merciful Mother, the Mother of all of you who live united in this land, and of all mankind, of all mankind, of all those who love me, of those who cry to me, of those who seek me, of those who have confidence in me. Here I will hear their weeping, their sorrow, and will remedy and alleviate their suffering, necessities, and misfortunes. And so that my intentions may be made known, you must go to the house of the bishop of Mexico and tell him that I sent you and that it is my desire to have a sanctuary built here.[350]

Following Mary's request, Juan went to the house of the recently named bishop of New Spain (Mexico), Don Juan de Zummaraga. The bishop met with Juan Diego and told him to return in a few days. The next time the two met, the bishop asked Juan Diego to bring back a sign indicating that Mary had appeared on the Tepeyac Hill. In the apparition, and fourth and last one, that followed Juan Diego's meeting with the bishop, Mary instructed Juan Diego to gather up Castilian roses that were miraculously flowering during the cold of winter on the hill of Tepeyac. Juan Diego obeyed,

---

[350] Catherine Odell, *Those Who Saw Her: Apparitions of Mary, Updated and Revised* (Kindle Edition: Our Sunday Visitor, 2010), Location 549-564.

and gathered the roses into his tilma. When he met with the bishop, Juan Diego displayed the roses not knowing that upon the tilma was displayed a full size portrait of an Aztec looking Mary complete with dark black hair. This miracle, coupled with the title Mary chose to identify herself with, were sufficient signs for the bishop and he agreed to build a Church on the Tepeyac Hill. The reason why Mary is titled Our Lady of Guadalupe is due to a vision of Mary Juan Diego's uncle had. In describing the vision to Juan Diego, the uncle said:

> I, too, have seen her. She came to me in this very house and spoke to me. She told me that she wanted a temple to be built at Tepeyac Hill. She said that her image should be called "Holy Mary of Guadalupe," though she did not explain why.[351]

The title appealed to the bishop, since he was from Spain and knew of a devotion in Spain to Our Lady of Guadalupe. Her Spanish title and her Aztec appearance were two ways by which Mary universally invited all people, of all ethnicities, into a deeper relationship with her son Jesus.

On December 26, 1531, at the first procession of the tilma from the bishop's church to the recently built chapel on Tepeyac Hill, Mary brought differ-

---

[351] Catherine Odell, *Those Who Saw Her: Apparitions of Mary, Updated and Revised* (Kindle Edition: Our Sunday Visitor, 2010), Location 657-661.

ent people together in yet another way. During the procession, according to accounts, the Aztec natives engaged in a mock battle during which one Aztec died after being hit by an arrow to his neck. Upon being placed in front of an image of Our Lady of Guadalupe, the man regained his life, and sat up. All that remained of his neck wound was a scar.[352]

This miracle, along with Mary's miraculous appearances to Juan Diego, led millions of Aztecs and other Mexicans to convert to Catholicism. In addition, many of the millions of pilgrims to the 1976 most recent Basilica of Guadalupe also have been experienced conversions.[353] Currently, the universal Church celebrates the feast of Our Lady of Guadalupe on December 12th, and the St. Juan Diego's feast day on December 9th.

If interested in the historical sources upon which the above narrative is based, read the January 23, 2002 article from the *L'Osservatore Romano* titled, "Our Lady of Guadalupe: Historical Sources."[354] The sources identified include written

---

[352] Catherine Odell, *Those Who Saw Her: Apparitions of Mary, Updated and Revised* (Kindle Edition: Our Sunday Visitor, 2010), Location 669-676.

[353] Carl Anderson, *Our Lady of Guadalupe: Mother of the Civilization of Love* (New York: Doubleday, 2009), 6-20.

[354] L'Osservatore Romano, "Our Lady of Guadalupe: Historical Sources" ewtn.com, https://www.ewtn.com/library/MARY/LADYGUAD.HTM, (accessed June 19, 2016). "Recent research and discoveries have confirmed the ancient data of a constant "*traditio*" of Guadalupe from the 16th century, and even lead to the confirmation of the actual existence of Juan Diego. Among them, we recall the study on the *Escalada Codex*

(chronicles, annals, devotions etc.), oral, and archaeological accounts.

Our Lady of Laus

The following century, Mary was reported to having appeared between the years 1664 and 1718 in Laus, France, to the young, teenage shepherdess, Venerable Benoîte (Benedicta) Rencurel. Despite disagreement among Church officials on the validity of the apparitions, including during the life time of Benedicta who was even placed under house arrest for fifteen years,[355] Bishop Jean-Michel de Falco of Gap gave his approval to the apparitions on Sunday, May 4th, 2008, during a mass celebrated in the French Alps town of Laus.

The bishop said, "I recognize the supernatural

(found by the Spanish Jesuit Xavier Escalada and presented on 31 July 1997), that includes the death certificate of Juan Diego Cuauhtlatoatzin, with the signatures of Antonio Valeriano and of the friar, Fr Bernardino de Sahagún. Other discoveries that confirm the historical truth of Guadalupe are the 17th-century documents found in the archives of the ancient *Convent of Corpus Christi* in Mexico City, still unpublished, that refer to certain legal proofs of "purity of blood", or to the noble lineage of two candidates to the monastic life who declared they were descendants of the visionary, Juan Diego."

[355] Catherine Odell, *Those Who Saw Her: Apparitions of Mary, Updated and Revised* (Kindle Edition: Our Sunday Visitor, 2010), Location 843. Odell explains that when Benedicta was placed under house arrest, France was suffering from Jansenism which erred by overemphasizing, with respect to grace and God's mercy, original sin, mortal sin, and predestination.

origin of the apparitions and the events and words experienced and narrated by Benedicta Rencurel. I encourage all of the faithful to come and pray and seek spiritual renewal at this shrine." He further added, that while "nobody is obliged to believe in apparitions...but if they help us in our faith and our daily lives, why should we reject them?"[356]

In her numerous apparitions to Benedicta, Mary as a "reconciler and "refuge for sinners" urged her to "pray continuously for sinners," and beseeched all to repent specifically by going to confession. Mary requested that when priests fulfill her request in hearing the confessions of pilgrims to Laus, that they do so with gentleness, and not with

---

[356] "Vatican Recognizes Marian Apparitions in France," Rome, Italy, May, 5, 2008, catholicnewsagency.com, http://www.catholicnewsagency.com/news/vatican_recognizes_marian_apparitions_in_france/, (accessed June 19, 2016). Interestingly, according to the prominent French Catholic philosopher Jean Guitton, "the shrine of Laus is one of the most hidden and powerful shrines of Europe." Guitton was a friend of Pope Paul VI who invited Guitton to be an observer at the Second Vatican Council. Catherine Odell, *Those Who Saw Her: Apparitions of Mary, Updated and Revised* (Kindle Edition: Our Sunday Visitor, 2010), Location 881; "Vatican Recognizes Marian Apparitions in France," Rome, Italy, May, 5, 2008, catholicnewsagency.com, http://www.catholicnewsagency.com/news/vatican_recognizes_marian_apparitions_in_france/, (accessed June 19, 2016); Eric Pace, "Jean Guitton, 97, Philosopher, Author and Friend of Popes," March 27, 1999, nytimes.com, http://www.nytimes.com/1999/03/27/arts/jean-guitton-97-philosopher-author-and-friend-of-popes.html, (accessed June 19, 2016).

harshness. Currently, confessions are heard at Laus by the clergy of the diocese with the help of the community of the Brothers of St. John.[357] Pilgrims are also invited to apply oil from a sanctuary lamp on their wounds with the hope of miraculous healing promised by Mary to Benedicta.

Our Lady of the Miraculous Medal

On July 18, 1830, St. Catherine Labouré says she was awakened at night by the voice of a child calling her to the chapel of her Daughters of Charity motherhouse convent at 140 Rue du Bac, Paris. There, Mary told her, "My child, God wishes to entrust a mission to you. It will be the cause of great suffering to you...You will be contradicted, but do not fear, grace will be given to you. ... The times are very evil. ... The whole world will be upset by evils of every kind..."[358] Throughout the year, Mary continued to appear to Catherine. During the apparition of November 27, 1830, Mary requested Catherine make stamp medallions according to an image revealed to Catherine.

---

[357] Vatican Recognizes Marian Apparitions in France," Rome, Italy, May, 5, 2008, catholicnewsagency.com, http://www.catholicnewsagency.com/news/vatican_recognizes_marian_apparitions_in_france/, (accessed June 19, 2016); Catherine Odell, *Those Who Saw Her: Apparitions of Mary, Updated and Revised* (Kindle Edition: Our Sunday Visitor, 2010), Location 783, 798.

[358] Catherine Odell, *Those Who Saw Her: Apparitions of Mary, Updated and Revised* (Kindle Edition: Our Sunday Visitor, 2010), Location 952-959.

The image included the Blessed Mother standing on a globe, twelve stars, the Sacred Heart of Jesus, the Immaculate Heart of Mary and the letter M placed on top of a cross, and the words "O Mary! Conceived without sin, pray for us who have recourse to thee!'" The following year, Catherine, through her confessor Father Aladel, finally received permission from a local archbishop for the medallions to be made. In 1836, the apparitions of Labouré received official approval by the bishop of Paris. From this time until today, over a billion of the miraculous medals have been made and distributed.[359]

360

---

[359] Catherine Odell, *Those Who Saw Her: Apparitions of Mary, Updated and Revised* (Kindle Edition: Our Sunday Visitor, 2010), Location 885-1101.

[360] Xhienne, "Medal of the Immaculate Conception (aka Miraculous Medal), a medal created by Saint Catherine

Our Lady of La Salette

On September 19, 1846, Mary was reported to have appeared once again in France to two children, Maximin Giraud and Melanie Calvat. Maximin, age eleven, and Melanie, age fourteen, worked as cowherds in the Alps. On September 19th, 1846, as they were leading cows and one goat to pasture Mary appeared to them.[361]

On the fifth anniversary of the apparitions, Bishop de Bruillard of Grenoble approved of the apparitions in a pastoral letter. He wrote, "We judge that the Apparition of the words of the Blessed Virgin to the two cowherds on the 19th of September,1846, on a mountain of the chain of Alps, situated in the parish of La Salette, in the archpresbytery of Corps, bears within itself all the characteristics of truth and that the faithful have grounds for believing it indubitable and certain."[362] Melanie's account of the Marian apparitions were published with the approval (imprimatur) of yet

---

Labouré in response to a request from the Blessed Virgin Mary who allegedly appeared rue du Bac, Paris, in 1830. The message on the recto reads: "*O Mary, conceived without sin, pray for us who have recourse to thee — 1830*"," photograph, https://commons.wikimedia.org/wiki/File%3AMiraculous_me dal.jpg, (accessed June 19, 2016).

[361] Catherine Odell, *Those Who Saw Her: Apparitions of Mary, Updated and Revised* (Kindle Edition: Our Sunday Visitor, 2010), Location 1103-1287.

[362] Catherine Odell, *Those Who Saw Her: Apparitions of Mary, Updated and Revised* (Kindle Edition: Our Sunday Visitor, 2010), Location 1266.

another bishop, Bishop Zola. Excerpts from her account are below:

> "...The next day, the 19th of September, I met Maximin on the way up. We climbed up the mountain side together. ... Maximin told me to teach him a game. ...We began to feel sleepy and having moved a couple of feet away, we went to sleep on the grass. ... When I woke up I couldn't see the cows, so I called Maximin and climbed up the little mound. From there I could see our cows grazing peacefully and I was on my way down, with Maximin on his way up, when all at once I saw a beautiful light shining more brightly than the sun.
>
> "Maximin, do you see what is over there? Oh! my God!" At the same moment, I dropped the stick I was holding. Something inconceivably fantastic passed through me in that moment, and I felt myself being drawn. I felt a great respect, full of love, and my heart beat faster.
>
> I kept my eyes firmly fixed on this light, which was static, and as if it had opened up, I caught sight of another, much more brilliant light

which was moving, and in this light I saw a most beautiful lady sitting on top of our Paradise, with her head in her hands.

This beautiful Lady stood up, she coolly crossed her arms while watching us, and said to us:

"Come, my children, fear not, I am here to PROCLAIM GREAT NEWS TO YOU."

These soft and sweet words made me fly to her, and my heart desired to attach itself to her forever. When I was up close to the Beautiful Lady, in front of her to her right, she began to speak and from her beautiful eyes tears also started to flow.

"If my people do not wish to submit themselves, I am forced to let go of the hand of my Son. It is so heavy and weighs me down so much I can no longer keep hold of it. I have suffered all of the time for the rest of you! If I do not wish my Son to abandon you, I must take it upon myself to pray for this continually. And the rest of you think little of this. In vain you will pray, in vain you will act, you will never be able to make up for the trouble I have taken over for the rest of you.

I gave you six days to work, I kept the seventh for myself, and no one wishes to grant it to me. This is what weighs down the arm of my Son so much.

...

The priests, ministers of my Son, the priests, by their wicked lives, by their irreverence and their impiety in the celebration of the holy mysteries, by their love of money, their love of honors and pleasures, the priests have become cesspools of impurity. Yes, the priests are asking vengeance, and vengeance is hanging over their heads. Woe to the priests and to those dedicated to God who by their unfaithfulness and their wicked lives are crucifying my Son again! The sins of those dedicated to God cry out towards Heaven and call for vengeance, and now vengeance is at their door, for there is no one left to beg mercy and forgiveness for the people. There are no more generous souls, there is no one left worthy of offering a stainless sacrifice to the Eternal for the sake of the world.

God will strike in an unprecedented way.

Woe to the inhabitants of the

earth! God will exhaust His wrath upon them, and no one will be able to escape so many afflictions together.

The chiefs, the leaders of the people of God have neglected prayer and penance, and the devil has bedimmed their intelligence. They have become wandering stars which the old devil will drag along with his tail to make them perish. God will allow the old serpent to cause divisions among those who reign in every society and in every family. Physical and moral agonies will be suffered. God will abandon mankind to itself and will send punishments which will follow one after the other for more than thirty-five years.

...

France, Italy, Spain, and England will be at war. Blood will flow in the streets. Frenchman will fight Frenchman, Italian will fight Italian. A general war will follow which will be appalling. For a time, God will cease to remember France and Italy because the Gospel of Jesus Christ has been forgotten. The wicked will make use of all their evil ways. Men will kill each other, massacre each other even in their homes.

...

The earth will be struck by calamities of all kinds (in addition to plague and famine which will be wide-spread). There will be a series of wars until the last war, which will then be fought by the ten Kings of the Antichrist, all of whom will have one and the same plan and will be the only rulers of the world. Before this comes to pass, there will be a kind of false peace in the world. People will think of nothing but amusement. The wicked will give themselves over to all kinds of sin. But the children of the holy Church, the children of my faith, my true followers, they will grow in their love for God and in all the virtues most precious to me. Blessed are the souls humbly guided by the Holy Spirit! I shall fight at their side until they reach a fullness of years.

... Many convents are no longer houses of God, but the grazing-grounds of Asmodeas and his like. ....[363]

---

[363] "Modern History Sourcebook: Apparition of the Blessed Virgin on the Mountain of La Salette the 19th of September,

Our Lady of Lourdes

About ten years later, in 1858 it was reported that a heavenly lady, thought to be Mary, was repeatedly appearing in France at a grotto in Lourdes, near the Pyrenees, to a fourteen-year-old peasant girl, St. Bernadette Soubirous. At first, Mary did not reveal her identity to Bernadette telling her "It is not necessary."[364] In a later apparition, on Wednesday, February 24th, Mary told Bernadette that she wanted "Penitence" from others and that people "Pray to God for the conversion of sinners."[365] The following day, Thursday, February 25th, Mary asked Bernadette to do penance by kissing the ground and then told her to dig up the ground with her fingers.

When Bernadette obeyed Mary's additional request to drink water from the mud that Bernadette just had scraped and eat a nearby growing plant, people thought she was mad. The following day, the local police commissioner forbade Bernadette from returning to the grotto. Then, on March 1st of that same year Catherine Latapie partially paralyzed hand was healed after she placed it in the water that was flowing out of the site where Bernadette had

1846," legacy.fordham.edu, https://legacy.fordham.edu/halsall/mod/1846sallette.asp, (accessed June 19, 2016).

[364] Catherine Odell, *Those Who Saw Her: Apparitions of Mary, Updated and Revised* (Kindle Edition: Our Sunday Visitor, 2010), Location 1380.

[365] Catherine Odell, *Those Who Saw Her: Apparitions of Mary, Updated and Revised* (Kindle Edition: Our Sunday Visitor, 2010), Location 1410.

scrapped mud apart. Miracles of healing up until today have also occurred in relationship to the water from the grotto.

The day after the miracle, March 2nd, Mary asked Bernadette that priests arrange processions and build a chapel near the grotto. Finally, on March 25th, the feast of the Annunciation, Mary revealed her identity as "I am the Immaculate Conception."[366] Only four years earlier on December 8th, 1854, Pope Pius IX had dogmatically defined the Immaculate Conception, a title and teaching Bernadette had never heard before, but the local priest had. When Bernadette told the priest what title the heavenly lady had identified herself as, his belief that Mary was appearing to Bernadette solidified.[367] A few years later, in 1862, Bishop Laurence, the Bishop of Tarbes, gave his official approval to the eighteen apparitions of Mary to Bernadette. In his document he declared:

> We judge that Mary Immaculate, the Mother of God, really did appear to Bernadette Soubirous, on eighteen occasions from 11th February 1858 at the Grotto of Massabielle, near the town of Lourdes; that these Appari-

---

[366] Catherine Odell, *Those Who Saw Her: Apparitions of Mary, Updated and Revised* (Kindle Edition: Our Sunday Visitor, 2010), Location 1468.

[367] Catherine Odell, *Those Who Saw Her: Apparitions of Mary, Updated and Revised* (Kindle Edition: Our Sunday Visitor, 2010), Location 1294-1555.

tions bear the characteristics of truth ; that the faithful can believe them as true. We humbly submit our judgement to the judgement of the Sovereign Pontiff, who is responsible for governing the Universal Church.[368]

Our Lady of Pontmain

On January 17th, 1871, yet another Marian apparition occurred in France at Pontmain during the Franco-Prussian War. The first to see the apparition was the twelve-year-old boy Eugene Barbadette. Mary appeared to him as he was helping his father at night in their barn. When he pointed out the apparition of a beautiful woman smiling down upon him, his younger brother also was able to see the apparition, which his father could not see. When others were called over, only the children could see Mary. A crowd began to form. Once again, none of the adults, including the parish priest, could see the apparition. The children saw Mary dressed in a blue gown, covered by gold stars that multiplied. Words appeared beneath her, "But pray, my children. God will hear you in a little while. My Son allows Himself to be touched."[369]

---

[368] "The Recognition: 1862," enlourdes-france.org, http://en.lourdes-france.org/deepen/apparitions/the-recognition, (accessed June 19, 2016).

[369] Catherine Odell, *Those Who Saw Her: Apparitions of Mary, Updated and Revised* (Kindle Edition: Our Sunday Visitor, 2010), Location 1637-1650.

Upon hearing the children read the message aloud, the crowd rejoiced and, according to the children, so did Mary. Her expression of joy changed to sorrow, however, when the people began singing the hymn "My Sweet Jesus." As she mourned, a large red cross with the image of Jesus on it appeared in her hands. The cross, though, disappeared and Mary once again became joyful before shortly afterwards disappearing. The apparition lasted three hours.

The same evening of the apparition, the Prussians ended their advance on Laval, the capital of French region that included the small farming village of Pontmain. According to some Prussian soldiers, they also had seen a vision of "A Madonna...guarding the country and forbidding us to advance."[370] Eleven days later, the Prussians withdrew all their troops from France, and, shortly afterwards, signed an armistice with France. The following year, on February 2, 1872, the local bishop of Laval, Bishop Wicart, approved the apparition.[371]

Our Lady of Knock

On August 21, 1879, a Marian apparition took

---

[370] Catherine Odell, *Those Who Saw Her: Apparitions of Mary, Updated and Revised* (Kindle Edition: Our Sunday Visitor, 2010), Location 1663.

[371] Catherine Odell, *Those Who Saw Her: Apparitions of Mary, Updated and Revised* (Kindle Edition: Our Sunday Visitor, 2010), Location 1560-1686.

place by the Knock Parish of Knock, Ireland. It was witnessed by fifteen townspeople of Knock. Unlike many other Marian apparitions, both children and adults saw this apparition. In the apparition, Mary's appearance was accompanied by St. Joseph, St. John the Evangelist, angels, an altar, a cross and a lamb. An artistic representation of the vision at Knock may be seen below. No words were reported being spoken. While this vision has not received direct approval by the Irish bishops, the bishops have not discouraged pilgrims from going to Knock. Notable visitors to the shrine at Knock include John Paul II in 1979, and Mother Teresa of Calcutta in 1993.[372]

373

---

[372] Catherine Odell, *Those Who Saw Her: Apparitions of Mary, Updated and Revised* (Kindle Edition: Our Sunday Visitor, 2010), Location 1694-1826.

[373] EamonnPKeane at English Wikipedia, "Knock Shrine," photograph, https://commons.wikimedia.org/wiki/File%3AKnock_shrine.JPG, (accessed June 20, 2016).

Our Lady of Fatima

Beginning on May 13th 1917, on the thirteenth day of six consecutive months, apparitions of the Blessed Mother were seen by three shepherd children: Lúcia dos Santos and her cousins Jacinta and Francisco Marto. As reported by Avelino de Almeida in the October 17th, 1917, edition of the Portuguese newspaper, *O Século*, during the sixth and last apparition, "Before the astonished eyes of the crowd, whose attitude carries us back to biblical times and who, full of terror, heads uncovered, gaze into the blue of the sky, the sun has trembled, and the sun has made some brusque movements, unprecedented and outside of all cosmic laws-the sun has 'danced,' according to the typical expression of the peasants..."[374]

Two other notable apparitions occurred on July 13th. On this day, Mary showed the children a vision of hell and then assured the children that those on their way to damnation could be saved by reparation and devotion to the Immaculate Heart of Mary. However, she warned "if people do not cease offending God, a worse one [war] will break out[375]:

You have seen hell where the souls of

---

[374] William T. Walsh, *Our Lady of Fatima* (New York: Doubleday, 1954), 147.

[375] William T. Walsh, *Our Lady of Fatima* (New York: Doubleday, 1954), 147; Catherine Odell, *Those Who Saw Her: Apparitions of Mary, Updated and Revised* (Kindle Edition: Our Sunday Visitor, 2010), Location 1977.

poor sinners go. To save them, God wishes to establish in the world devotion to my Immaculate Heart. If they do what I will tell you, many souls will be saved and there will be peace. The war is going to end. But if they do not stop offending God, another and worse one will begin in the reign of Pius XI. When you see a night illuminated by an unknown light, know that it is the great sign that God gives to you that he is going to punish the world for its crimes, by means of war, of hunger, and of persecution of the Church and of the Holy Father. To prevent this, I come to ask for the consecration of Russia to my Immaculate Heart, and the Communion of reparation on the first Saturdays. If they listen to my requests, Russia will be converted, and there will be peace. If not she will scatter her errors throughout the world, provoking wars and perse-cutions of the Church. The good will be martyrized; the Holy Father will have much to suffer; various nations will be annihilated. In the end, my Immaculate Heart will triumph. The Holy Father will consecrate Russia to me, and she shall be converted, and a certain period of peace will be granted to the world.[376]

Our Lady of Beauraing

Between 1932 and 1933, Marian apparitions were seen by five children, all under the age of sixteen, in Beauraing, Belgium. According to the children, Mary identified herself as "the Immaculate Virgin" and requested that all pray. In the final vision, Mary asked the oldest child, Fernande, age fifteen, if she loved her son, and if she loved her. Fernande responded yes to both questions. Upon hearing this, Mary told her, "Then sacrifice yourself for me."[377] The apparitions were approved on July 2nd, 1949, by the local Bishop of Namur. A number of healings have been credited to Our Lady of Beauraing.[378]

Our Lady of Banneux

The same year that Marian apparitions were reported in Beauraing, another eleven-year-old Belgian girl, Mariette Beco, reported seeing Mary. According to Mariette, Mary identified herself as

---

[376] William T. Walsh, *Our Lady of Fatima* (New York: Doubleday, 1954), 81-82.

[377] Catherine Odell, *Those Who Saw Her: Apparitions of Mary, Updated and Revised* (Kindle Edition: Our Sunday Visitor, 2010), Location 2334.

[378] Catherine Odell, *Those Who Saw Her: Apparitions of Mary, Updated and Revised* (Kindle Edition: Our Sunday Visitor, 2010), Location 2113-2373.

the "Virgin of the Poor", told her that, "I come to relieve suffering"[379] and requested that a chapel be built. Similar to the apparition at Pontmain, Mary appeared smiling. Similar to the apparition at Lourdes, Mary directed Mariette to a spring that brought about miraculous healings. On August 22, 1949, the Bishop of Liege gave his approval to the apparitions.[380]

Our Lady of Akita

In 1973, in Akita, Japan, Marian apparitions were reported by Sister Agnes Katsuko Sasagawa. The apparitions were accompanied by a statue of Mary that bled from the hand and wept. About ten years later, in a 1984 pastoral letter, the local bishop of Niigata, Bishop John Shojiro Ito, approved the apparitions as worthy of belief and gave his authorization for the veneration of Our Lady of Akita.[381] His approval and authorization

---

[379] Catherine Odell, *Those Who Saw Her: Apparitions of Mary, Updated and Revised* (Kindle Edition: Our Sunday Visitor, 2010), Location 2480-2486.

[380] Catherine Odell, *Those Who Saw Her: Apparitions of Mary, Updated and Revised* (Kindle Edition: Our Sunday Visitor, 2010), Location 2547.

[381] Catherine Odell, *Those Who Saw Her: Apparitions of Mary, Updated and Revised* (Kindle Edition: Our Sunday Visitor, 2010), Location 2565-2875. A of the notable private revelations to Sister Agnes are as follows. "The blood shed by Mary has a profound meaning. This precious blood was shed to ask for your conversion, to ask for peace, in reparation for the ingratitude and the outrages toward the Lord. As with devotion to the Sacred Heart, apply yourself to devotion to the most

followed the 1978 *Norms Regarding the Manner of Proceeding in the Discernment of Presumed Apparitions or Revelations*, issued by the Congregation for the Doctrine of the Faith. According to the Norms, the local bishop has the primary responsibility for determining if an alleged apparition is worthy or belief or not. Below, are two pertinent excerpts from this document that were made public on December 14, 2011. Prior to this date, only bishops had access to these norms:[382]

When Ecclesiastical Authority is

Precious Blood. Pray in reparation for all men. Say to your superior that the blood is shed today for the last time. Your pain also ends today. Tell them what happened today. He will understand all immediately. And you, observe his directions...The work of the devil will infiltrate even into the Church in such a way that one will see cardinals opposing cardinals, bishops against other bishops. The priests who venerate me will be scorned and opposed by their confreres ... churches and altars sacked; the Church will be full of those who accept compromises, and the demon will press many priests and consecrated souls to leave the service of the Lord. The demon will be especially implacable against souls consecrated to God. The thought of the loss of so many souls is the cause of my sadness. If sins increase in number and gravity, there will no longer be pardon for them." Catherine Odell, *Those Who Saw Her: Apparitions of Mary, Updated and Revised* (Kindle Edition: Our Sunday Visitor, 2010), Location 2680-2684, 2740-2745,

[382] "Norms Regarding the Manner of Proceeding in the Discernment of Presumed Apparitions or Revelations," campus.udayton.edu, http://campus.udayton.edu/mary/NormsApparitionsMadePublic_2.html, (accessed June 20, 2016).

informed of a presumed apparition or revelation, it will be its responsibility:

a) first, to judge the fact according to positive and negative criteria (cf. *infra*, no. I);

b) then, if this examination results in a favorable conclusion, to permit some public manifestation of cult or of devotion, overseeing this with great prudence (equivalent to the formula, "for now, nothing stands in the way") (*pro nunc nihil obstare*).

c) finally, in light of time passed and of experience, with special regard to the fecundity of spiritual fruit generated from this new devotion, to express a judgment regarding the authenticity and supernatural character if the case so merits.

...

III. AUTHORITIES COMPETENT TO INTERVENE

1. Above all, the duty of vigilance and intervention falls to the Ordinary of the place.

2. The regional or national Confer-

ence of Bishops can intervene:

a) If the Ordinary of the place, having done his part, turns to it to judge the matter with greater certainty;

b) If the matter pertains to the national or regional level; always, however, with the prior consent of the Ordinary of the place.

3. The Apostolic See can intervene if asked either by the Ordinary himself, by a qualified group of the faithful, or even directly by reason of the universal jurisdiction of the Supreme Pontiff (cf. *infra*, no. IV).[383]

Our Lady of Kibeho

From 1981 to 1989, Marian apparitions to schoolchildren were reported in Kibeho of southwestern Rwanda. The apparitions, which included both Mary and Jesus speaking to the children, seem to have predicted the 1994 Rwandan genocide

---

[383] "Norms Regarding the Manner of Proceeding in the Discernment of Presumed Apparitions or Revelations," February 25, 1978, Vatican.va, http://www.vatican.va/ roman_curia/congregations/cfaith/documents/rc_con_cfaith _doc_19780225_norme-apparizioni_en.html, (accessed June 20, 2016).

perpetrated by the Hutus against the Tutsi and Hutu moderates. Within the span of only one hundred days, 800,000 Rwandans were massacred, sometime by their neighbors. Many of the victims were hacked to death with machetes. Some were blown up in Churches they were hiding in.[384]

Other messages included Mary exhorting people to pray, convert, and cease breaking the first and sixth commandment. With the respect to the sixth commandment, the twenty-two-year-old student Agnes Kamagaju reported that Jesus in August of 1982 told her that the youth "should not use their bodies as an instrument of pleasure. They are using all means to love and be loved, and they forget that true love comes from God. Instead of being at the service of God, they are at the service of money. They must make of their body an instrument destined to the glory of God and not an object of pleasure at the service of men. They should pray to Mary to show them the right way to God."[385] The apparitions to three of the schoolchildren received approval from the local bishop in 2001.[386]

---

[384] "Rwanda: How the Genocide Happened," bbc.com, http://www.bbc.com/news/world-africa-13431486, (accessed June 20, 2016).

[385] Catherine Odell, *Those Who Saw Her: Apparitions of Mary, Updated and Revised* (Kindle Edition: Our Sunday Visitor, 2010), 3149-3162.

[386] Catherine Odell, *Those Who Saw Her: Apparitions of Mary, Updated and Revised* (Kindle Edition: Our Sunday Visitor, 2010), Location 3058-3297.

Our Lady of the Rosary of San Nicolas

On May 22, 2016, Bishop Hector Cardelli of San Nicolas in Argentina's Buenos Aires province announced at the conclusion of a mass held at the shrine of Our Lady of the Rosary of San Nicolas:

> [I]n my twelfth year of pastoring San Nicolas and, having followed with faith and responsibility the Marian events that I have known about since the very beginning, I have reached the decision to recognize them for my diocese. I recognize the super-natural nature of the happy events with which God through his beloved daughter, Jesus through his Most Holy Mother, the Holy Spirit through his beloved spouse, has de-sired to lovingly manifest himself in our diocese.[387]

The supernatural events the bishop was referring to took place between 1983 and 1990 to the middle-aged grandmother, Gladys Herminia Quiroga de Motta. Gladys received numerous mes-sages from Jesus and Mary as well as the stig-

---

[387] "A Marian Apparition Has Been Approved in Argentina – and It's a Big Deal," catholicnewsagency.com, http://www.catholicnewsagency.com/news/a-marian-apparition-has-been-approved-in-argentina---and-its-a-big-deal-31979/, (accessed June 20, 2016).

mata.[388] After carefully evaluating Gladys and her writings, a commission, established by Bishop Castagna, released a positive report on October 25, 1985. The report concluded the following:

> • There were no theological difficulties (or errors) in any of the writings of the visionary. In fact, one report said the messages were truly in harmony with Holy Scripture.
>
> • Because some medical data for a cure said to be connected with the claimed apparitions was missing, no conclusion could be made about it. On the other hand, serious testimonies in defense of the supernatural nature of the healing had been received and noted.
>
> • There was no evidence of psychopathological disorder or hallucination in the visionary, Mrs. Motta. Her personality seemed well balanced and in perfect harmony with reality.[389]

---

[388] Catherine Odell, *Those Who Saw Her: Apparitions of Mary, Updated and Revised* (Kindle Edition: Our Sunday Visitor, 2010), 3306-3573.

[389] Catherine Odell, *Those Who Saw Her: Apparitions of Mary, Updated and Revised* (Kindle Edition: Our Sunday Visitor, 2010), 3542-3548.

Application of Marian Teaching

Marian teaching contained in Scripture, taught by the magisterium and supplemented, in a non-obligatory manner, by private revelation is to have a practical moral effect of growth in love of God and of neighbor. As the Mother of God and the Mother of the Church, Mary repeatedly calls us to grow in this two-fold love by knitting us together as one body of Christ. In order to understand how Mary brings us together by encouraging the formation of true love relationships, her universal motherhood needs to be distinguished from physical mother-hood. Mary's universal motherhood of the Church is only analogously similar to physical motherhood, and, consequently, contains important differences. The noted Jesuit, Henri De Lubac in *The Mother of the Church* brings out both the important differences in this analogy by writing:

> The Church is not a mother "in the way Eve was"; she does not give birth to a people "whose birth would be a tearing away and the source of innumerable oppositions", as has been witnessed in all of history since the beginning. Quite the contrary, through childbirth, her goal is to react tirelessly against this misery that is congenital to our sinful race and to "gather into a single body the dispersed children of God". That is

what is expressed in a paradoxical image: whereas in the physical order, the child leaves the womb of his mother, and withdrawing from her, becomes increasingly independent of her protective guardianship as he grows, becomes stronger and advances in years, the Church brings us forth to the new life she bears by receiving us into her womb, and the more our divine education progresses, the more we become intimately bound to her. St. Irenaeus was already saying "one must cling to the Church, be brought up within her womb and feed there on the Lord's Scripture." St. Cyprian says in his turn: "Anyone who withdraws from the womb of the mother can no longer live and breathe alone: he loses the substance of substance of salvation." In his charity he also expresses this wish: "If possible, let none of our brothers perish! Let our joyous mother hold enclosed within her womb the unified body of a people in full harmony.[390]

Growth in love of God and neighbor, according to Henri de Lubac's reasoning, necessarily entails

---

[390] Henri De Lubac, *The Motherhood of the Church,* trans. Sergia Englund (San Francisco: Ignatius Press, 1982), 68-70.

becoming more "intimately bound" to Mary, to the Church. When the Marian, motherly dimension of the Church is lost sight of argues von Balthasar:

> ...Christianity threatens impercepti-bly to become inhuman. The Church becomes functionalistic, soulless, a hectic enterprise without any point of rest, made unfamiliar by the planners. And because, in this mainly-masculine world, all that we have is one ideology replacing a-nother, everything becomes pole-mical, critical, bitter, humorless, and ultimately boring, and people in their masses run away from such a Church.[391]

In another writing, von Balthasar even more strongly asserted that:

> The Marian understanding of the Church is the most decisive contrast to a merely organizational or bureaucratic concept of Church. We cannot make the Church, we must be Church. And it is only to the degree in which faith stamps our being more than our doing, that we are

---

[391] Brendan Leahy, *The Marian Profile* (New York: New City Press, 2000), 166. In reference to *Elucidations*, 112.

Church, that Church is in us. It is only in Marian being that we become Church. In her origins the Church was not made, but born.[392]

In a book that he co-authored with von Balthasar, Ratzinger similarly argued:

In my opinion, the connection between the mystery of Christ and the mystery of Mary ... is very important in our age of activism, in which the Western mentality has evolved to the extreme. For in today's intellectual climate, only the masculine principle counts. And that means doing, achieving results, actively planning and producing the world oneself, refusing to wait for anything upon which one would thereby become dependent, relying rather, solely on one's own abilities. It is, I believe, no coincidence, given our Western, masculine mentality, that we have increasingly separated Christ from his Mother, without grasping that Mary's motherhood might have some significance for

[392] Brendan Leahy, *The Marian Profile* (New York: New City Press, 2000), 198. In reference to "Die Ekklesiologie des Zweiten Vatikanums," *Internationale Katholische Zeitschrift Communio* 15 (1986), 41-52, espec. 52.

theology and faith. This attitude characterizes our whole approach to the Church. We treat the Church almost like some technological device that we plan and make with enormous cleverness and expenditure of energy. Then we are surprised when we experience the truth of what Saint Louis-Marie Grignon de Montfort once remarked, paraphrasing the words of the prophet Haggai, when he said, "You do much, but nothing comes of it!" (Hag 1:6) When making becomes autonomous, the things we cannot make but that are alive and need time to mature can no longer survive.[393]

Heeding the above advice, may we take to heart the Marian teachings we have received in our minds so that we will grow in love of God and neighbor as Mary knits us together as a mystical body, with Christ as the head.

---

[393] Joseph Ratzinger, Hans Urs von Balthasar, trans. A. Walker *Mary: the Church at the Source* (San Francisco: Ignatius Press, 2005), 16.

Discussion Questions

1. After doing some research, compare and contrast three Marian apparitions in specific ways. Include the following in your response: location, children, adults, messages, appearance of Mary, historical context, approval of the Church.

2. After carefully reading the 1978 *Norms Regarding the Manner of Proceeding in the Discernment of Presumed Apparitions or Revelations,* summarize the norms. Include the following in your response: reason for the norms, criteria for judging, competent authorities, intervention.

3. Discuss why von Balthasar and Ratzinger maintain that a Marian understanding of the Church helps in preventing a hyper-bureaucratic concept of the Church. Include in your answer the following: the Church and Mary as Mother, receptivity, and activity.